CATCHING FIRE

The Story of Firefighting

🔥 Dave Albright holds a cat rescued from a fire in a fifth-floor apartment. Even today, when emergency services can't always roll out to rescue pets, a lot of animals still owe their lives to the fire department. They get rescued, they get oxygen, and sometimes CPR is administered to a small, furry chest.

CATCHING FIRE

The Story of Firefighting

Gena K. Gorrell

Tundra Books

Published in Canada by Tundra Books, *McClelland & Stewart Young Readers*,
481 University Avenue, Toronto, Ontario M5G 2E9

Published in the United States by Tundra Books of Northern New York,
P.O. Box 1030, Plattsburgh, New York 12901

Library of Congress Catalog Number: 98-61435

Canadian Cataloguing in Publication Data

Gorrell, Gena K. (Gena Kinton), 1946-
    Catching fire : the story of firefighting

Includes bibliographical references and index.
ISBN 0-88776-430-4

1. Fire extinction – Juvenile literature.   2. Fire extinction – History – Juvenile
literature.   3. Fire fighters – Juvenile literature.   I. Title.

TH9148.G67 1999   j363.37   C98-932236-X

We acknowledge the support of the Canada Council for the Arts and the Ontario
Arts Council for our publishing program.

We acknowledge the financial support of the Government of Canada through the
Book Publishing Industry Development Program for our publishing activities.

Design by Ingrid Paulson
Printed and bound in Canada

1 2 3 4 5 6   04 03 02 01 00 99

I can imagine (if I were a little younger and had much better eyesight) being a police officer; I think I could accept occasional danger as part of that important job.

I can imagine (if I were a little younger and a lot stronger) being a paramedic, and helping people in risky situations.

But I don't understand how anyone can be a firefighter, and stand face to face with the age-old threat of fire — not just once in a while, as an accidental happenstance, but as an ordinary day's work.

I don't know how firefighters have the courage to do their job, but I'm grateful that they do, and I admire them very much. And that's why I wanted to write this book.

G.K.G.

CONTENTS

CATCHING FIRE

The Story of Firefighting

THE TIGER ON THE HEARTH

Half a million years ago, a small tribe of primitive creatures – not quite human, but almost – huddle inside their cave. Outside lie darkness and the damp chill of a rainy autumn night. Outside wait the teeth and claws of night-hunting beasts. But between the tribe and the fears and dangers of the dark is an amazing, magical guardian: a hot, bright fire.

In those days before people were people, what did early humanoids think as they watched the yellow flames dance, as they felt their faces glow in the warmth? They knew how to keep a fire going; they used it to harden the tips of their wooden hunting spears, and to cook the meat the hunters brought home. Yet what was it? Where did it come from? And when it "went out," where did it go?

Keep your distance, treat it with respect, and fire would do wonderful things for you. Get a little too close, or the least bit careless, and it could sear you with terrible pain, and mark you for life – perhaps even for death.

And sometimes – why? – a great fury of fire would sweep across the land, gobbling up trees and grass, and animals, and anyone it could catch, leaving nothing behind but stinking black ruin.

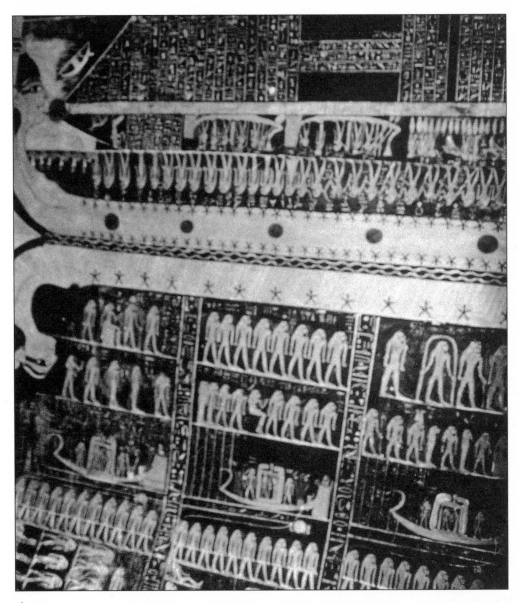

In the past, many people reassured themselves with stories about where the sun went at night. One Egyptian myth said it was swallowed by Nut, the sky goddess, each night, and reborn from her each morning. This ceiling painting shows the sun moving through Nut's body, hour by hour.

🔥 Helios, a sun god in classical Greece, drove his chariot and four fiery horses across the sky each day. Many early cultures believed that fire was a gift from the gods. The Greeks said that Prometheus stole it from Mount Olympus, the home of the gods, and gave it to man, and that he was brutally punished by Zeus, the king of the gods, for daring to give away such a precious treasure.

What was this ageless, bodiless being that came from nowhere and disappeared into nowhere? What kind of creature or spirit would slumber so tamely on your cooking-hearth, yet turn on you savagely, with no warning, for no reason?

Worshipping fire

We call those early humanlike creatures *Homo erectus*, because they stood erect on two legs, as we do. They evolved into our own species, *Homo sapiens* –

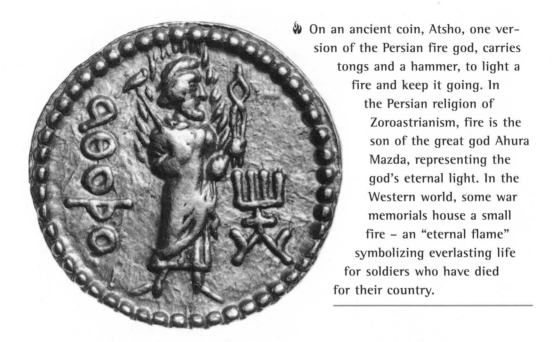

🔥 On an ancient coin, Atsho, one version of the Persian fire god, carries tongs and a hammer, to light a fire and keep it going. In the Persian religion of Zoroastrianism, fire is the son of the great god Ahura Mazda, representing the god's eternal light. In the Western world, some war memorials house a small fire – an "eternal flame" symbolizing everlasting life for soldiers who have died for their country.

"thinking people," as we have proudly named ourselves. Over the centuries, we have certainly spent a lot of time thinking about fire.

Early civilizations wondered about the glowing disc that rose in the eastern sky each morning, bringing warmth and light and security to the whole land. Was the sun something like the humble cooking fire, which brought those same comforts to a family? Would the sun burn you like a fire if you got too close? Could it – worse yet – some day go out, the way cooking fires sometimes did, leaving you in the cold and the dark forever?

People also wondered about the warmth they felt in their own bodies, and in so many animals. Where did it come from, and why did it eventually go out, just like a fire? What was the connection?

And what about the needles of fiery light that flashed from the sky during thunderstorms? What about the fountains of fire that spewed out of the earth itself, when a volcano erupted? What about those terrifying times of eclipse, when the sun disappeared for a while and broad daylight turned into night?

FIERY WORDS

The ancient Greeks had another theory about fire. They decided that everything in the world was made up of a few basic substances, or *elements*. The solid part of the world was earth; the wet part was water; the gas part was air. Since they needed something to explain warmth and life, they decided that the fourth element must be fire.

The Greek word for "fire" – πυρ, or "pyr" in our spelling – is a root of many English words, such as "pyre" (a bonfire lit on purpose, sometimes to cremate a body), "pyrotechnics" (fireworks), and "antipyretic" (medicine against fever).

The Latin word for "fire," *ignis*, is the root of our words "ignite" (set fire to) and "ignition." When we turn a key in a car's ignition, we are creating a spark of fire to burn the fuel that will move our "chariot" to the supermarket.

What was behind all these alarming mysteries?

In their search for an answer, many people came to worship the sun as a powerful god who rode across the sky each day, beaming down the blessings of heat and warmth on the world. Some societies decided that the sun also lent a spark of its fire to earthly creatures, giving them the magical warmth we call "life." As for the fire on the hearth, they judged it to be an earthly symbol of the god's power, a sacred reminder of the purity and generosity of the immortal sun god.

But the swift violence of fire was a warning that this great god had a temper. Sacred or not, fire could do terrible damage. Since they had little understanding of fire and how to control it, many people tried to please the sun god by praying, making sacrifices, or setting up statues and temples.

THE FABULOUS PHOENIX

The magical, eternal aspect of fire is beautifully imagined in the phoenix. This mythical red bird – there is only one – lives for five hundred years, and then sets fire to its own nest, singing itself a funeral hymn. When the fire dies, all that's left is an egg – and out comes the next phoenix.

Working with fire

However sacred fire might be, it was also remarkably useful. In time, people learned to melt down metals and mix them together into stronger, more workable alloys, and to pour the hot liquid metal into molds to shape tools and weapons. They built ovens so that food could be cooked slowly and evenly, without being watched all the time. They built kilns so that clay could be baked into long-lasting bricks and cooking pots. They made oil lamps and candles so they could carry light around their homes to wherever it was needed. They discovered that, by taking silica out of sand and melting it, they could create a miraculously transparent material — glass. Daily life was becoming more civilized and comfortable — and fire was an important part of it.

🔥 The Indian fire god Agni is crowned with flames. He is often painted in fiery colors, with red skin, yellow eyes, and black clothes. His two heads represent the two sides of fire – the useful and the destructive. He carries a fan for fanning the flames, an ax, a torch, and a ladle.

But at the same time, people were becoming even more vulnerable to fire. Now that they lived in towns and cities, in houses furnished with cloth and wood, with supplies of burnable products like oils, one small mistake could set off a fire that demolished hundreds of homes. With two-story buildings, and walls and gates and staircases, there was more risk of people being trapped in a fire. And because people had more property – more clothes and ornaments, more tools and toys – they had more to lose. Running away from a blaze was no longer enough; they wanted to know how to prevent fires, and how to put them out quickly if they started.

FIRE IN THE BIBLE

In the Bible, fire is often connected with divinity. In the book of Exodus an angel appears to Moses in a burning bush, and God is a pillar of fire leading the Israelites through the desert night. The book of Deuteronomy warns that "the Lord thy God is a consuming fire," and hell is described as a fire that can't be extinguished. When three virtuous young men, Shadrach, Meshach, and Abednego, are cast into a fiery furnace, their faith in God protects them from the flames. Some religions still use fire to purify people, or to test their goodness.

"PUT THE WET STUFF ON THE RED STUFF"

How fires start

Fire is a kind of chemical process called *combustion*: **fuel** and **oxygen** combine to produce **heat**, **light**, and **Xame**.

Fuel is anything that burns. Oxygen is a gas that makes up about one-fifth of the air we breathe; we need oxygen to live, and so does fire. But before fuel and oxygen can burst into flame, the fuel has to be hot enough to begin turning into a gas. It's this gas – not the solid fuel – that actually burns.

Different materials burn at different temperatures. The temperature something burns at is called its *ignition point* or *kindling point*. When something has a low ignition point, so it burns very easily, we say it's *flammable* – though really anything that burns is flammable.

The more oxygen there is in the air, the more easily a fire will start. Oxygen is used in some workplaces, like hospitals and welding shops, and the people who work with it have to be especially careful to prevent accidental fires.

Materials made up of small pieces, like twigs or loose papers, burn more easily than solid things like logs or books. If we want to burn a log in a fireplace, we don't light a match and hold it to the log; the log is large and dense, and the match probably won't heat it to its ignition point. Instead, we surround the log with paper and *kindling* (loose, dry sticks). The match warms the very

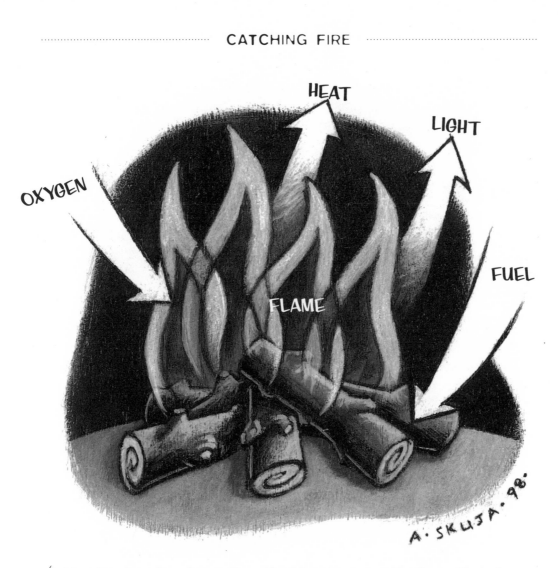

🔥 Most burning takes place in the yellowish outer part of the flame. The yellow color comes from tiny, glowing bits of soot (carbon). A clean flame – from natural gas, for example – has no soot, and glows blue.

flammable paper and kindling to their ignition point, and then the heat from the burning paper and kindling slowly warms the log until it too catches fire.

Though many gases don't burn, those that do tend to be very flammable. For instance, gasoline fumes catch fire much more easily than liquid gasoline.

That's why there are signs in gas stations warning people not to smoke around the pumps – with gasoline being pumped into cars, there are fumes in the air.

Since water is not flammable, very wet things don't burn. But if something wet is put in a fire, the heat evaporates the water – and when the material dries out, it will burn as usual. This is how forests catch fire. Even a tiny spark can set fire to dry leaves and bushes. And once that spark becomes a blaze, it can spread to the damp, shady parts of the forest, because it has enough heat to dry them out so that they too will burn.

How fires are stopped

Since a fire can burn only if it has fuel, oxygen, and heat, there are three basic ways of putting out a fire:

1. Take away the fuel.
2. Take away the oxygen.
3. Take away the heat.

Since the fuel is already on fire, we can't usually take it away; that would be dangerous. But sometimes we can take away fuel that the fire hasn't yet reached. Suppose a field of grass is on fire not far from a barn. The farmer may dig a wide ditch in the dry grass between the blazing field and the barn. If the fire can't cross the ditch of bare earth, it will run out of fuel before reaching the barn.

Taking away the oxygen is often much easier. If someone's jacket catches fire, you can throw a rug or blanket over the person. If an oily pan flames up over a campfire, you can pour a bucket of sand over it. In both cases you're cutting off the air so the fire can't breathe.

But the most common way of stopping a fire is to cool the fuel below its ignition point, so it's not hot enough to burn. And usually the easiest way to cool it – and to smother it at the same time – is to pour on water. Some firefighters call this "putting the wet stuff on the red stuff" – that's how simple the idea is.

🔥 As this town burns in the Middle Ages, the homeowners rescue their valuables and lower their children to safety. A bucket brigade passes pails of water up a ladder to the amateur firefighter brave enough to stand on the roof over the blaze. Bucket brigades are still used today, when there are no pumps and hoses at hand.

Of course, there's still one problem – how do you get the water to the fire? First you have to bring it from a source – maybe a lake, river, or ocean – and then you have to get it right into the heart of the fire, wherever it's most needed. If the roof of a house is on fire, pouring a bucket of water on the floor isn't going to help much!

❦ This bridge, taller than an eight-story building, used to be part of a great aqueduct carrying water to the Spanish city of Tarragona. It was built about two thousand years ago, when Spain was part of the Roman Empire.

Ancient cities, ancient fires

More than two thousand years ago, a man named Ctesibius, who lived in Alexandria, an Egyptian city on the shore of the Mediterranean Sea, invented a device for pumping water up into fires. Unfortunately his design was lost, and the fire pump wasn't reinvented until about five hundred years ago. In the centuries between, firefighting remained primitive. Early fire hoses were made from the intestines of oxen. When no pumps and hoses were available, buckets of water were passed from hand to hand by a bucket brigade, and when the blaze was above street level there was sometimes no way to get the water up to it. As a result, many cities suffered terrible destruction.

15

One of history's most famous fires was in ancient Rome. The city seemed well prepared for fire. It was renowned for its fine water supply; water was carried overhead by huge stone channels called *aqueducts*, and distributed to homes through a complex plumbing system. As far back as two thousand years ago, Rome had about seven thousand paid firefighters, equipped with ladders that fit together in sections, and jumping pillows to break the fall of people leaping from burning buildings. When they weren't putting out fires, these *vigilum cohortes* patrolled the city and punished people who broke the fire regulations. Yet in the first century A.D. a terrible fire wiped out half the city, and even destroyed seventeen of the aqueducts.

Another famous fire was in Alexandria. Whenever a ship docked there, the captain had to lend the city all the books on board, for copying, before the ship could leave. By this strategy the city built up a library of more than 700,000 books – an astounding number in the days before printing, when every book had to be copied by hand. But fire struck in the fourth century A.D. and much of the library was burned. Many great books were lost forever; we know they existed, but no copy has survived.

The cities fight back

In the 1600s – over a thousand years after the catastrophe at Alexandria – there still wasn't much hope of extinguishing a fire once it got out of hand.

THE ORIGINAL CURFEW

When parents today talk about a *curfew* of eight o'clock or ten o'clock, they mean that they expect their children safely home by that time. The word comes from medieval France, where the *couvre-feu* ("cover-fire") was the hour when all the fires in town had to be put out, or at least covered, so people could sleep without fear.

🔥 The Great Fire of London was in 1666, just fifty years after Shakespeare died. The blaze was spread by strong winds, and was fought with handheld syringes that shot about two quarts (liters) of water – pathetically feeble weapons against the inferno that raged through the narrow lanes and wooden houses for four days, and ate up most of the city. The king, Charles II, rode down with a pouch of gold coins to encourage the workers fighting the fire; he ended up wielding a spade and bucket himself, soaked and sooty in his fine clothes. Eventually barrels of gunpowder were used to blow up houses in the fire's path, robbing it of fuel.

When a house was insured against fire, a metal plaque called a *fire mark* was mounted on the outside. This was a guarantee to firefighters that they would be paid for their work. Rival fire brigades would race to claim a blaze as their own – but if it turned out there was no fire mark, the building might be left to burn.

Firefighting equipment included ropes, wooden or leather water buckets, salvage bags for rescuing a few valuables, and tools such as axes, saws, and long-handled hooks. The tools were used in a hasty effort to pull down neighboring buildings before the fire got to them, to starve it of fuel.

Since property owners couldn't stop the spread of fire, they began buying fire insurance to pay for their losses. Fire insurance companies soon realized that they would save a lot of money if they could find better ways to stop fires, instead of just paying for the damage afterward. The companies led the way in developing better equipment and paying teams of firefighters – though the firefighters were supposed to save only the houses of paid-up customers!

Machines replace muscle

The first fire engine, developed around 1650, was no more than a water tub that was filled from buckets and a pump that was worked by hand. Because this machine had only a short nozzle, it had to be placed very close to the fire. Despite its limitations, it could shoot a steady stream of water into the fire – far more effective than a series of bucketfuls.

Before long, fire pumps like these were put in wooden boxes on wheels, so they could be rolled to the fire scene. Leather fire hoses came into use, though they were expensive because they had to be sewn by hand, like fine shoes. With a hose attached to the pump, the people operating the pump could stay at a safer distance from the fire.

🔥 Not long before the Great Fire of London, this pump was in use in Holland. The tank was filled by hand, and the men on the left are pumping the water manually. The machine didn't deliver a lot of water, but it was the first step toward our modern fire engines.

In 1808 riveted leather hoses were invented to replace the expensive sewn ones. Soon after, a hose-reel was developed, so that long lengths of coiled hose could be transported. By the 1820s, rubber hoses were coming into use; they were later replaced by fabric hoses.

In 1829 the first steam-driven fire engine was invented. There was a curious paradox here: fire was used to heat water, to turn it into steam, and then the

⚗ This hose reel, built in 1838, looks a bit like Cinderella's carriage, but it's a well-designed piece of machinery. Note the bells at the front, set off by the vehicle's movement, and the lantern at the back – a more sedate version of today's siren and flashing lights.

steam was used to pump water to put out fire! In 1870 an aerial-ladder wagon was invented, so firefighters could reach upper stories and the victims trapped there. The next year a hose-elevator was introduced, to save them carrying the heavy hoses with them. By the 1870s, too, chemical fire extinguishers were coming into use.

As firefighting equipment improved, so did fire prevention. More and more rules were written about what materials could be used for building, and how heating and cooking fires had to be kept safe. As early as 1648 the governor

This print from 1861 shows primitive steam engines delivering powerful jets of water many stories up. Notice how many uniformed firefighters are shown; early North American cities were built largely of wood, and fire was a constant threat. In 1871, most of Chicago, Illinois, was wiped out by a fire that left hundreds dead and 90,000 homeless. That very same day, some 200 miles (320 km) to the north, the little lumber town of Peshtigo, Wisconsin, was swept away by a forest fire that killed 1,500 people and countless animals. Of Peshtigo's 400 buildings, only one wall of one house remained.

🔥 A steam fire engine and an aerial-ladder truck rush to a fire in 1897. These gleaming vehicles were likely the town's pride and joy. Although firefighters started using steam engines to pump water in the early 1800s, they still relied on horses to pull their equipment, right into the twentieth century.

of New Amsterdam (now New York) hired fire inspectors to fine people who disobeyed the regulations. In 1820 the city of York (now Toronto) ordered every householder to

Keep Two Buckets for carrying water, when any House shall happen to be on Fire . . . [and] keep two Ladders, the one to reach from the Ground to the Eaves of the House, the other to be properly secured and fixed with Hooks or Bolts on the roof near the chimney. . . .

UP, LADDERS!

A poem from 1912 catches the frantic drama of a fire scene. One verse reads:

"Up, ladders!" Brawny axemen broke
The panes and plunged through flame and smoke
To save, perchance, a chair, a cloak,
    A hat or gingham gown.
Some hurled from windows chinaware
And costly glass and pictures rare;
While other-some, with tender care,
    A mattress lowered down.

The towns and cities were changing too. Early firefighters had relied on wells, lakes, and rivers for their water. When no source was at hand, water had to be rushed in by water-tank wagons. Now more and more communities had piped water supplies, and some also had hydrants, above-ground pipes with nozzles where fire crews could tap into the water supply. (The first hydrants were just holes in the water pipes, sealed with removable plugs. That's why hydrants are also called "fireplugs," or just "plugs.") With plenty of water being steam-pumped through hundreds of feet of hose, fire crews were no longer fighting a losing battle. They were becoming the heroes who saved the day. They were good at their job, and they were proud of it.

Even with all their equipment and expertise, firefighting remained a daunting job. A news report from 1904 tells how a raging fire gobbled up warehouses and offices, and then leapt across the street toward the firemen and their engines:

Horses could not stand the heat that human beings forced themselves to endure. The firemen working right in under this canopy of flames

🔥 When this house burned, less than a hundred years ago, water still had to be brought by bucket brigade and carried up ladders to the roof. There was plenty of bravery involved, but not much hope of saving the building.

dragged back their hoses and . . . the ponderous fire fighting machines were yanked back to safety by a score of tugging firemen.

The firemen quickly attached their equipment to the next hydrant back, but soon that too was engulfed by the blaze, as building after building was swallowed up. As heavy winds scattered the water from their hoses, the firemen moved dangerously close to try to douse the flames.

A wall tottered. A hoarse shout of warning went up from a hundred keen-eyed spectators. Every man held his breath until, one by one, the imperilled firemen, rolling and tumbling in their haste, broke through the wall of smoke.

Today we have a scientific understanding of fire, and much more advanced ways of controlling and extinguishing it. But in our modern world of chemicals and high-rises, airplanes and subway trains, the job of firefighting is still a dangerous one – and it's more complicated than it ever was before.

BEATING THE "RED DEVIL"

You're going to see a play in a big new theater. You edge your way into the mass of people inching across the wide marble lobby, and slowly the crowd files into the theater itself. As you shuffle down the packed aisle, you look at all the people wedging them-selves and their coats and bags into the rows of seats, and suddenly you wonder what would happen if there was a fire. How could all these people ever find their way out in time?

Don't worry — you're not the first person to think of this. Buildings nowadays have to meet a strict fire code that defines some of the measures we use to protect ourselves against the "red devil," as fire is sometimes called. Some precautions are *passive* — they are just there, like fireproof walls — and others, like sprinklers and alarms, become *active* if there's a fire. Some work against the flames, and others control the spread of deadly smoke. If you look around, you'll spot some of these precautions.

How many exit doors do you see? There are rules about how many doors the building needs, based on how many people are allowed inside. And those doors can't be too far apart, or too close together either. They have to be near enough that everyone can reach one, but spread out enough that a single fire can't block them all. They have to be wide enough to let frightened people get out quickly. They may have to swing outward, rather than inward, so they can't be blocked by a panicky crowd.

You can probably see glowing EXIT signs over the doors, to remind you which way to go. There will also be emergency lighting to help you find your way. (You may be able to see lights mounted over the doors, like spotlights or giant flashlights.) Both of these have to run off a separate power supply (such as a battery) in case fire cuts off the electricity.

But just having lots of doors isn't enough. If the doors led into a wide-open part of the building, people trying to escape might have to get through smoke and dangerous gases. So if a fire door doesn't take you straight outdoors, the rules usually say it has to lead through a walled passage (maybe a stairwell) that will hold the smoke back.

If there aren't enough separate passages to let people out, the building may have outdoor fire escapes — usually metal stairways. These have to be placed away from windows, so they can't be blocked by the smoke and flames pouring out. Some buildings have escape chutes, like giant waterslides without the water. Others have portable fire ladders that can be hung from windows if they are ever needed.

The building has to have *fire separations* — walls, floors, and ceilings designed to slow down the spread of fire and smoke. In a theater there's often an asbestos

MAXIMUM CAPACITY . . .

Have you ever seen a sign — perhaps in a restaurant or meeting hall — stating how many people are allowed in the room? Many fire precautions are based on the number of people who would have to escape in an emergency. The number of people permitted depends on the size of the room and also on the likelihood of fire; for example, an office is allowed more people than a hotel kitchen of the same size.

fire curtain to shut off the backstage area in case a fire starts there. The materials used in the building may have been rated for *combustibility*; the carpets, curtains, even the paint on the walls, can be tested for how quickly they burn, and whether they give off dangerous gases.

You've probably noticed that some buildings have glass-fronted cabinets containing fire equipment. The hose inside is connected to a *standpipe*, a pipe that runs to the local water supply. Someone who spots a very small fire can open this cabinet and use the hose and extinguisher to put it out. (For most fires, call the fire department and get everyone out of the building. Too many people have died trying to put out a "small fire.")

🔥 Some people keep a fire ladder or fire rope at home to be sure they'll be able to escape if the building burns. In a more sedate age, this elegant contraption of chains and pulleys served the same purpose.

An engineer at Underwriters Laboratories – a safety-testing organization – rates roofing shingles for fire resistance. This particular exercise checks how high winds affect the burning shingles. Tests like these make sure products are safe for their intended use.

When we use products in unusual ways, we need to remember that they haven't been tested for this. For example, for a New Year's party at a pub, ten people dressed up as Bo-Peep and her sheep. The nine "sheep" had homemade costumes of cotton batting glued onto black leotards. But the glue was highly flammable. One sheep brushed past a lighted cigarette, and the whole flock was soon in flames. Fortunately the pub owner kept his wits and grabbed a fire extinguisher, but seven people went to hospital, just because they forgot about fire safety.

WHAT IS ASBESTOS?

Asbestos is a mineral (like a rock). It comes in various forms, but the kind we mean here comes in silky threads that are easily woven into fabric. Because it's strong and very fire-resistant, asbestos was popular for years for fireproofing. It's used less these days because we know now that breathing asbestos dust can be unhealthy.

If the building is tall, the pressure in the water supply won't be strong enough to force water up to the top floors. In that case the standpipe leads to a two-sided *siamese connection* outside the building. The sprinkler system is attached to another siamese connection. Two hoses on a pumper engine are attached to the two water intakes of each siamese connection, and the truck pumps the water up to where it's needed.

Many buildings have an elevator for firefighters to use. (It's marked with a sign – maybe a little fire helmet.) Most modern elevators go to the ground floor and shut down when the fire alarm goes off, to stop people from trying to use them, and perhaps getting trapped. But a firefighter elevator is set up so that fire crews can override this, and use it to move their heavy gear up toward the fire. Of course, they can't risk taking the elevator all the way to a blaze, but at least they can get within a few floors of it.

Fire code standards have been developed over centuries, and are always changing. These days, computers are being used to improve the standards. Real fires are set in dummy rooms, and the spread of heat, smoke, and gas is tracked by cameras and sensors. Next, virtual buildings are constructed on a computer, and the information from the real fires is used to predict what anti-fire measures will be needed in each building. Researchers have even done tests on sleeping people, to see how quickly different fire alarms could wake them up.

It's not only the inside of the building that gets checked. Before the plans are approved, the site is checked for emergency access. Are the nearby roads

WHAT HAPPENS IF YOU BREATHE SMOKE?

Smoke inhalation is dangerous in a lot of ways:

🔥 Fire burns up the oxygen in air; breathing smoky air with little oxygen can make us tired, dizzy, even unconscious.

🔥 The heat and dirty particles in smoky air can damage the delicate tissues inside our breathing passages.

🔥 Since many materials give off chemical fumes when they burn, smoky air may contain poisons that affect the brain and nervous system.

🔥 Smoky air is hard to breathe. When people have trouble breathing, they are more likely to panic — and less likely to act sensibly to save themselves.

wide enough and straight enough to let fire trucks through? Is there anything overhead that might block their way? In other words, long before the building goes up, experts are already asking themselves exactly what will happen if there's ever a fire.

Spreading the word

Of course, before we can get people out of a burning building, we need to know there's a fire; and then we need a way to warn people, and to call for help.

We have detectors that sense smoke and set off an alarm that can be heard anywhere in the building. We have manual pull alarms (usually small red boxes on the wall) so anyone who spots a fire can warn other people in the building; sometimes the alarm also notifies the fire department. We have portable fire extinguishers so that very small fires can be put out on the spot. Sprinklers may be built into the ceiling, connected to the water system below by a vertical standpipe, to shower water down on the fire. Some buildings have extraction fans to blow smoke and fumes outdoors. Many have a public-address system so somebody in charge can talk to people, calming them down and telling them what to do.

Who makes sure all these rules are obeyed?

Since the chief of a fire department is busy running the day-to-day operations of the fire crews, there's often somebody else – perhaps a fire marshal or fire commissioner – working on a more general level. This official oversees jobs like investigating fires, researching their causes, collecting statistics, and administering fire regulations. The fire marshal or fire commissioner is often in charge of a large area, such as a whole state or province.

THE GREAT FIRE OF WINDSOR

While new buildings are designed with extensive fireproofing, sometimes it's impossible to protect an old building without destroying its historic character. In 1992, Windsor Castle – home of the kings and queens of England for almost a thousand years – caught fire around midnight, when workers left a spotlight turned on too close to a curtain. The ancient timbers and flammable materials caught fire like matchsticks, and with the open stairwells, and no fire doors to block the blaze, the fire spread rapidly. It took 14 hours of frantic work, 225 firefighters, 39 fire vehicles and a million gallons of water to put out the fire. Although hundreds of volunteers and emergency workers had formed a human chain to pass priceless paintings and treasures out of the burning castle, precious pieces were destroyed, and the building was damaged terribly.

But things still go wrong

Because our fear of fire is so deep-rooted, many people panic when they hear the call "Fire!" In their terror they forget about being sensible; they may even forget where the doors are. There are painful stories of people dying because they ran the wrong way, or were trampled by others, or made a thoughtless mistake – like pulling frantically on a door, tugging and tugging, when a push would have opened it. In a famous American fire in 1942, at the Cocoanut Grove nightclub in Boston, almost five hundred people died. Bodies were

🔥 Even fire preparations can be done with a sense of humor. This steel plate in a Tokyo sidewalk covers a fire hydrant.

stacked four or five deep in front of the two revolving doors. Fire officials said three hundred lives might have been saved if the doors had been designed to swing outward.

Sometimes, fire precautions are ignored because people have their minds on other problems. In England, for example, people organizing a rugby game were afraid fans might sneak in without paying, so they locked and chained the gates once the game had started. They were also afraid fans might riot and use anything heavy as a weapon, so they took away the fire extinguishers. When a dropped cigarette started a small fire in garbage under the stands, there was no way to fight it and no way to get out. Fifty-six people died.

Hurray, here come the fire trucks!

As we stand helpless before a burning building, we greet the arrival of the fire department with relief and excitement. *They'll know what to do! They'll get this blaze under control! They'll dash in and rescue anybody trapped inside!* But behind those masks, under those heavy helmets, firefighters are just people like the rest of us. How did they get this job? How did they learn what to do? And why do they take on the daunting job of walking into fire when most of us can only think of running away?

Many, of course, are drawn by the excitement and challenge, and even the risk. Some are following family tradition; they've grown up hearing stories from relatives in the fire service. They've hung around the fire hall, wondering at the tools and trucks. They've seen people come home reeking of smoke, exhausted, even injured, but triumphant in their success.

"We see people lose everything. Sometimes we see how what we do makes a difference," explains experienced firefighter Ron Kyle. "We see lives end, and sometimes — delivering babies — we see lives begin." "No matter what you're doing, you're trying to help somebody," says Jason Verlaan. "There are days when you see bad stuff, but at least you know you've done your best. That's why we're always training, always practicing what we've learned." Peter Seagrove, a recruit fresh from the fire academy, says, "It's the best job in the world."

Who gets to be a firefighter?

It's not easy to make the grade. No matter how advanced the equipment becomes, a lot of physical strength is still necessary. When firefighters enter a burning building, they wear about 100 pounds (45 kg) of equipment. They often have to walk up many flights of stairs, lugging heavy hoses and other tools. They have to rescue unconscious victims of all sizes, and drag or carry them to safety. They may even have to save a fallen partner loaded with another 100 pounds of gear!

Applicants are usually tested in a number of areas: general knowledge, overall health, psychological fitness, strength, endurance. Physical tests often mimic real-life rescues. Would-be firefighters may have to run an obstacle course while wearing full firefighting gear, drag a weighted duffel bag as heavy as a person, or carry a dummy up a ladder.

Those who are accepted study a host of subjects. They take basic courses before graduation, and they may come back for extra training after they've had some experience on the job. They have to know all about fire: how to prevent

THE BUTCHER, THE BAKER . . .

When the fire alarm sounds, it's not only full-time fire crews who respond. A gardener locks up her tools and runs for her truck; a student gobbles his sandwich as he jumps on his bike. These people are volunteer firefighters. When they get the call – perhaps by a town siren, perhaps by telephone or pager – they drop their normal lives to be part of the firefighting team. Some volunteer departments get intensive training and full equipment; others have only the basics. Some are paid an hourly rate for their time at a fire; others work for free. For every hundred full-time firefighters in the United States today, there are about three hundred volunteers.

🔥 Students in full gear practice putting out an oil fire. Notice that it takes several people to hold onto a hose, because the powerful jet of water makes it so hard to control. The heat and smoke of this exercise help prepare students for the real thing.

it, how it grows, how it reacts to air and water. They need to understand how buildings are constructed, how fire travels through different structures, and how construction materials react to heat and fire. They learn about the many kinds of doors, windows, and locks they may have to get through. They study *hydraulics*, to know how water behaves under high pressure, and how it's affected by height and distance. They learn to handle long, heavy hoses without letting them fold or tangle. They spend hours climbing up and down ladders, wearing heavy gear. They learn to deal with fires in high-rise buildings, working hundreds of feet above the street. They practice with all kinds of tools, from rope to axes to power saws. They learn first aid.

🔥 Crews practice fighting high-rise fires on a mock apartment building. The ladders are mounted on turntables so they can be rotated and raised in any direction. Because the high ladder makes the truck tippy, the vehicle is propped up by stabilizers at the midsection and rear, so it won't fall over.

The fire college usually has *burn buildings* and vehicles where instructors can set straw, wood, oil, or other fuels ablaze, so students can try putting out a variety of fires in realistic conditions. There's a *drill tower* where they can practice going up and down stairs with all their gear, carrying hoses and dummies as well. There may be a *smoke tower* that can be filled with harmless artificial

🔥 People with neck or back injuries have to be handled very carefully, to avoid spinal cord injuries that could leave them paralyzed. These veteran firefighters have come back to school to learn how to rappel down a steep cliff with a victim immobilized in a wire stretcher called a *Stokes litter*.

smoke; students are sent in to find their way around, while instructors put chairs and other obstacles in their path, or to search for hidden dummies and bring them out. When they've learned to maneuver with very little visibility, their face masks may be covered up so they can practice in total blackness. Then they may be sent through a maze of doors, windows, and tunnels – some so narrow that they can't fit through wearing their air tanks, and they have to take them off and push them through separately. In short, the training simulates as many real-life problems as possible.

Getting in and getting out

Firefighters are trained for a lot more than just fires. They learn *extrication* – how to remove victims (or themselves) from difficult, dangerous situations. They learn how to get people out of wells, sewers, tanks, and silos. They learn about elevators, and how to reach people trapped in them. They may take courses in rescuing people from mines and caves. They may become emergency medical technicians, with advanced first-aid skills. They may learn to rescue people caught in flooding rivers, or people who have fallen through ice. They may study *hazmat* – dealing with spills and fires of *haz*ardous *mat*erials like poisons and explosives. They may learn to do rope rescues, transporting victims across rivers or up cliffs, or to work in bomb and earthquake disasters, propping up walls and ceilings so they can rescue victims trapped below.

All this training is stressful and even frightening, but it's absolutely essential. Firefighters have to know how to save their own lives if things go wrong. And the more practice they've had, the less likely they are to panic when their lives – as well as ours – are on the line.

THE WHAT AND THE HOW

It's just an ordinary day, and you're strolling down the street. Ahead of you there's a girl walking a puppy, and a boy on a bicycle. Across the road two people are unloading shopping bags from a car. And in the distance — what's that? The hair stands up on the back of your neck even before you recognize the sound — sirens! Fire trucks, and they're coming closer, they're coming this way, they're coming RIGHT DOWN THIS STREET! Everybody stops to watch as the engines scream by. You see the drivers threading their way through traffic; you see the gear and tools that seem to fill every bit of space on the trucks; you see the firefighters in their turnout gear, their faces serious and tense. Where are they going? And what will they do with all that equipment when they get there?

When we think of fire trucks, we usually think of pumper engines and ladder trucks. But fire departments use lots of other vehicles: tankers, rescue vehicles, power units, high-rise units, and, of course, the fire chief's car. The equipment varies greatly from one community to another. A small town may have only one pumper engine and ladder truck; a large city will have as many specialized units as it can afford.

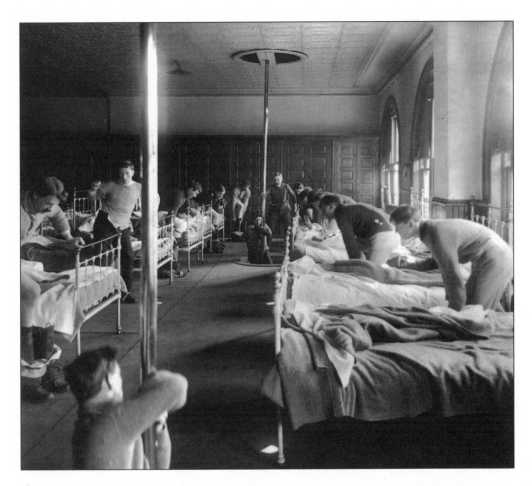

🔥 A fire crew of the past leaps out of bed for an emergency call. Notice that these men keep their boots and pants at the foot of the bed. Many fire halls still have brass poles connecting the floors, so firefighters upstairs can slide down quickly, instead of wasting time running down the stairs.

Pumper engines

These vehicles have powerful pumps to draw water from a source — a hydrant, a reservoir, a lake, even a swimming pool — and force it into hoses at high pressure, so a lot of water can be shot a long way.

🔥 A pumper stands in the station, ready to roll within seconds. Everything is set up for speed. Crew members still leave their turnout pants rolled down over their boots, ready to be jumped into, but now they keep them beside the truck; turnout coats are within grabbing distance. Helmets are inside the truck, to be put on during the trip. The tube hanging from the ceiling, on the left, is an exhaust to clear out diesel fumes while the truck sits in the fire hall.

The hose on a water pumper usually comes in lengths of 50 or 100 feet (15 or 30 m). A typical pumper might carry 400 feet (120 m) of small *attack hose* – the hose that fire crews usually carry into the fire – and three times that much *supply hose*, in a larger size, to deliver water to the attack hoses. It will also carry other widths – from ¾ inch (20 mm) to 6 inches (150 mm) – as well as an array of nozzles, adaptors, and tools.

A hose 1 ½ inches (38 mm) wide can deliver 155 gallons (almost 600 l) of water a minute – thirty times more than a garden hose – and the hose on an aerial ladder may deliver as much as 1,000 gallons (almost 4,000 l) a minute. *Pumper-tankers* have a large tank so they can bring their own water supply with them.

🔥 This fire crew from the early 1900s had to make do with a primitive hose-reel. Their protective clothing would fend off water, but not much else. Rumor has it that firemen like the one on the right would soak their beards in water before entering a blaze, or even stuff their beards in their mouths!

Some pumper engines have a small extra tank for making firefighting foam. Some engines are strictly *foam pumpers*, and don't pump plain water at all; they carry a mixture of water and concentrate that gushes into dense foam as it leaves the fire hose nozzle and meets the air. Foam puts fires out faster than water, and does less damage to property. It's also used to smother fires of materials like gasoline, which would only be spread by water.

Ladder trucks

Most ladder trucks these days are *aerial-ladder apparatuses*. This means they carry sections of ladder that extend automatically into a single length that may reach as high as seventeen stories. The aerial ladder is used to rescue people trapped

🔥 Raised above the blaze, the aerial tower becomes an observation post, giving a better view of what's going on. The firefighters on the left are trying to cut through the roof with a saw.

high in burning buildings, of course, but it's also the fire crew's staircase for getting up to where the fire is. A built-in hose called a *ladderpipe* lets them shoot water way into the heart of the fire. When an aerial-ladder truck is topped by a platform or bucket where several firefighters can stand and work, it's called an *aerial-platform apparatus*.

Because a long aerial-ladder truck can't get around tight corners, some trucks are *articulated*; they have two segments, front and back, so they can bend around a corner the way a train does. Articulated trucks have two drivers, one for the front and one for the back. The driver in the back has to remember to

ROPE TRICKS

We tend to think of rope as pretty boring stuff, but for firefighters it can mean life or death. They classify it as *dynamic* (stretchy, so it absorbs some of the shock of a fall) or *static* (not stretchy, and safer for most jobs). They also classify it as *life-safety* (for supporting rescuers and victims) or *utility* (for everything else). They learn the good and bad points of various rope fibers (cotton, nylon, polyester, etc.) and constructions (twisted, braided, and so on). They practice rope use, rope inspection, and rope maintenance. They learn to tie lots of different knots, and to use accessories such as a block and tackle (for lifting or pulling heavy loads), or a harness (for raising or lowering someone). In fact, "plain old rope" turns out to be a pretty complicated subject!

steer in the opposite direction from the driver in front, to swing the rear of the truck around corners.

What's the "hook" in "hook and ladder"?

Ladder trucks are sometimes called "hook and ladders," because they also carry fire-fighting tools such as hooks (or *pike poles*) for tearing down walls and ceilings. Some hooks are as long as 5 yards (meters), so they can reach up to smash second-floor windows. As well, the trucks carry rescue and first-aid equipment, and various kinds of rope.

Other fire vehicles

If the fire is very large, or is some distance from the nearest water source, a *hose wagon* may be sent in, to supply the extra hose needed.

If the fire is even farther from water, a *tanker* may be used to ferry water in. The water can be dumped into a folding, portable tank, and used to fight the fire while the tanker goes to fetch more.

🔥 Firefighter Todd Letwinka demonstrates a pike pole. The point jabs through the ceiling, and the hook pulls it down. The bottom of the pole is slanted so the firefighter can tell which way the hook is pointed, even in dense smoke. Notice all the portable ladders in the aerial-ladder truck. There are roof ladders, with curved ends that hook securely over roof peaks; attic ladders, short and narrow enough to be carried up cramped attic stairways; even ladders with steps that fold flat, so the ladder becomes no wider than a pole. Some ladders come with a heat sensor that changes color if the metal gets hot enough to be damaged.

If the emergency involves hazardous materials such as corrosive or poisonous chemicals, a *hazmat truck* may be sent. It holds special protective clothing and decontamination materials, and equipment for controlling leaks and spills. It has information about dangerous substances, and carries communications equipment so that, if the crew need to know more, they can contact a central library of hazmat data.

The hazmat truck also carries high-tech devices such as a *thermal detection gun* to identify hot areas, an *explosimeter* to warn of leaking natural gas, a *dosimeter* to measure radiation, and a monitor for deadly carbon monoxide gas. Other detectors measure poisonous and corrosive vapors, check that there is enough oxygen to breathe, and test for explosive gases (by sucking a little air into a chamber and trying to explode it).

Since a lot of water may be needed to flush away dangerous chemicals, the vehicle may be a *pumper/hazmat* combination.

A *rescue truck* is used for both fires and non-fire emergencies, such as people stuck in elevators or trapped in cars. It carries rope and other equipment for reaching victims, freeing them, removing them, and giving them first aid. It also carries everyday tools like mops, brooms, shovels, and tarpaulins, used to clean up and protect what's left of the building.

A *mobile command post* serves as headquarters during a fire. It has communications equipment, maps and floor plans, and other vital information. For example, it might have a floor plan of the burning building, a list of dangerous chemicals stored there, and the phone number of the building manager. It might have a plan of the area, with information about nearby hydrants, and whether any disabled people live in the neighborhood. A large command post may have computers, sleeping quarters, and its own power supply, so it can be used anywhere.

A *light and power unit* carries a larger power supply (a generator). It can light up the emergency scene with floodlights, provide electricity for power tools, and even supply emergency power to the building on fire. Some units also carry an air supply for the firefighters.

❧ Have you ever noticed that fire stations often have tall towers? They're not just for decoration. Crews coming back from a fire can hang their hoses from the tower to let them dry, so they don't get moldy. If the station doesn't have an elegant built-in tower like this one in Pennsylvania, a simpler tower may be built nearby, or the hose may be dried inside, on a drying rack.

Hoses can also be damaged by chemicals, too much sun, too much water pressure, or careless handling. They have to be folded and carried in specific ways, and inspected regularly. There are even special washing machines just for fire hoses.

A *high-rise truck* carries basic equipment like that on the other trucks, packed in portable modules that can be carried up into high-rise buildings. It also has a portable command post; if the fire is on the twentieth floor, for example, the *incident commander* can set up this command post a few floors below, and stay in close touch with the crews fighting the fire.

The *fire chief's car* usually carries the chief's own gear, extra air tanks and first-aid supplies, a radio, a telephone, maybe a computer, and whatever else the chief needs to take command of the fire scene. It may also carry detection devices like those on the hazmat truck.

Dressing for a fire

What firefighters wear depends on what they're doing. Basic *turnout gear* includes a protective coat and pants — designed to resist heat, cuts, and many chemicals — and heavy-duty boots reinforced with steel. There's a hood to cover the face and neck, and special heatproof gloves. Although this protection is necessary, it has its disadvantages. "You're not aware of how intense the heat is," points out Captain Ray Mattison. "You don't have that natural sense of what you're going into, because you're all covered up."

A rigid helmet protects the firefighter against heat, chemicals, and sharp or heavy objects. Its flip-up face shield covers the eyes, fabric flaps pull down to protect the ears, and a chin strap holds the helmet firmly in place. There may be a flashlight mounted on one side, and a radio tucked inside so the firefighter can stay in communication.

Other kinds of clothing are used for special purposes. Fire crews working with dangerous chemicals may wear *splash suits* to protect them against spills and splashes, or *encapsulating suits* that protect the whole body against highly dangerous chemicals. Since an encapsulating suit is rather like a giant plastic bag, firefighters need special training to work inside one. They also need help in getting the awkward suit on and off.

For an exceptionally hot fire — perhaps a chemical fire, or an airplane fire — there are several levels of suit. An *approach suit* has an aluminum surface that

🔥 The Nomex turnout gear in this advertising photo may not look elegant, but the science behind it is highly sophisticated. Suits are tested in real fire, on a thermal mannequin studded with heat sensors, while a computer checks for any spot hot enough to burn a firefighter. The suits have to protect fire crews against heat and injury, yet be light and flexible enough that they can still do a stressful, exhausting job, whether they're climbing ladders or crawling through crevices.

reflects heat, letting the wearer stand temperatures up to 2,000°F (over 1,000°C), but only for three minutes. A *proximity suit* has layers of insulation that let crews work in the heat for five minutes or more, but only in temperatures up to about 900°F (500°C). A *fire entry suit* lets a firefighter walk right into the heart of the flames, but it's very awkward to work in. It can be used

🔥 In the early 1900s a New York fireman invented this primitive breathing mask attached to an air hose. It was a small step in the right direction.

only for quick, simple tasks, such as entering a blazing chemical plant to shut off a valve and stop the chemical flow.

Most firefighters also carry a Personal Alert Safety System (PASS). That's a siren that makes a loud shrieking noise if the person collapses, or even stays still for a while. It can also be switched on manually by someone who needs help. The PASS sounds an automatic warning that somebody may be in deadly danger.

The tank on a firefighter's back is a *self-contained breathing apparatus* (SCBA), and it's filled with compressed air. It's like a diver's scuba tank ("scuba" stands for "self-contained *underwater* breathing apparatus") but it's worn the other way around, with the narrow end down, so the controls are easier to reach. The breathing mouthpiece attached to the tank is built into a face mask, and a little bit of air is always flowing into the mask — even between breaths — to keep smoke from seeping in from outside.

WHAT'S THE POINT OF COMPRESSING AIR?

We compress air to make it smaller, so we can carry it around. (It's the same idea as cramming a sleeping bag into a small suitcase.) If you take a little less air than a telephone booth holds, and run it through an air compressor, you can fit it into a tank small enough to carry on your back. That's enough air to last fifteen or twenty minutes when a firefighter is working hard and breathing heavily. (Tanks come in different sizes, for different kinds of work.)

Since we can't breathe compressed air — our lungs would blow up like balloons — a small *regulator* lets each breathful of air expand to its normal size before it flows out the mouthpiece.

A tool for every job

Because they're never sure what job they'll be facing till they get to it, fire crews carry tools to do just about anything. Some of their tools are *hydraulic* – meaning that an engine pumps fluid to make the tool work. Others are *pneumatic*, run by the force of compressed air. But most work by old-fashioned muscle-power.

They have shears, spreaders, and rams for ripping open things like doorways and vehicles. They have jacks and airbags for raising things – for example, a car

🔥 A flashlight can help you see in the dark, but it doesn't help in heavy smoke; it just lights up the smoke. One of the newest firefighting tools is this *thermal imaging camera* (TIC), which "sees" heat and turns it into a picture. A firefighter with a TIC can travel through a burning building in the thickest, blackest smoke, by picking out the heat patterns of doors and obstacles, and can track down the source of the fire by seeing the hot spots. The TIC can even lead rescuers to unconscious victims, locating them by their body heat. Some thermal imagers are light enough to be worn on a helmet, to leave the firefighter's hands free.

THE ABCs OF FIRE EXTINGUISHERS

Often, the fastest, simplest way to put out a small fire is to douse it with a fire extinguisher. Since there are different kinds of fires, there are different kinds of extinguishers. They're labeled by class, and sometimes also by capacity.

Class A fires involve materials like wood, paper, and plastic. Since they can be put out with water, some Class A extinguishers spray high-pressure water. Others spray a foam that helps the water soak into the fuel and cut off the oxygen.

Class B fires are of liquid, grease, or gas. It can be dangerous to put water on a Class B fire, because the water may spread the burning fuel. (Water poured on a pool of burning oil just makes the pool larger.) Class B extinguishers smother the fire.

Class C fires involve electricity, so putting water on them could create a danger of electrocution. Class C extinguishers smother the fire with foam or a dry chemical that doesn't conduct electricity. (The other choice is to cut off the electricity – by unplugging the burning equipment, for example – and then treat the fire as Class A.)

Class D fires are rare, and involve certain metals that burn at very high temperatures. There is a specific extinguishing material for each kind of burning metal. (To learn about using a fire extinguisher, see the chapter "Taming the Tiger.")

pinning a victim down. (An empty airbag is put under whatever has to be raised, and then inflated until it lifts the thing up. Some airbags are made of Kevlar, a strong synthetic fabric used in bulletproof vests, and can lift 75 tons, almost 70,000 kg – heavier than any truck normally allowed on a highway.)

They have axes and hatchets, chisels and saws, crowbars and sledgehammers. They have tools for prying things open – including the *Halligan tool*, a combination pick, claw, and prying tool invented by a firefighter. They have oxyacetylene torches for burning their way through metal, and special tools for forcing locks. They have assorted fire extinguishers.

A fire crew heading into a high-rise building may take along a *high-rise kit* containing a fire hose they can attach to a standpipe inside the building, since the hoses in standpipe cabinets may be old or inadequate. They may also carry a small pack of essential tools and first-aid equipment, since they're going to be a long way from the main supply on the truck.

One of the newest firefighting tools is a radio-controlled robot that carries hose into a blaze to spray water or foam. A thermal-imaging camera on the robot lets the operator direct this mechanical firefighter to where it's needed.

Year by year, firefighting tools, vehicles, and garments become safer and more sophisticated. The new technology is expensive, and most fire departments can't buy as much equipment as they'd like. But each generation of firefighters is better equipped than the one before.

"FIRE, FIRE, FIRE!"

It's Tuesday morning, and B platoon are on duty at Fire Hall No. 15. They've just finished their morning cleanup, and they're gathering in the lunchroom to organize their training schedule. While Brian puts the kettle on, Chris looks for the cookies he brought in yesterday. But before he finds them, a high-pitched clatter comes from the printer in the control room. The crew are on their feet even before they hear the two-tone BE-BOP of the alarm. They race for the trucks, Brian flicking off the stove as he passes, while a loud voice announces a fire reported in a house a dozen blocks away.

Imagine going through your day knowing that in two minutes – or even two seconds – you may have to drop everything and dash to an emergency. As you squeeze toothpaste onto your toothbrush, you know you may not have time to brush your teeth; as you butter the hot toast to go with your scrambled eggs, you know the meal may grow cold on the table. Although most of the day is routine, there's no telling what the next moment will bring.

In most North American cities today, calls for fire, police, or ambulance can be handled through a central system. When someone calls the emergency number (such as 911), the dispatcher decides what services are required, and tracks their location and activities through a computer system. If fire crews are

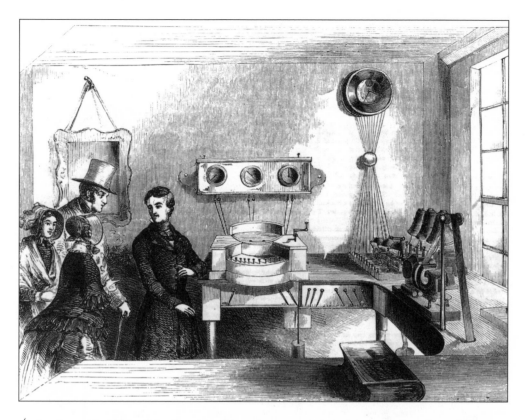

🔥 In the mid-1800s this elegant telegraph system pinpointed the location of Boston fires. In earlier days, bells on churches or town halls would be rung to announce the emergency. Later, *call boxes* mounted in the streets were connected to fire halls through a system using *ticker tape* (paper tape coded with punched holes).

ONE ALARM, TWO ALARM, THREE . . .

Each fire department has its own rules about how many vehicles it sends to a fire of a certain size. In a large city, a one-alarm fire might call for two pumpers, one aerial-ladder truck, and a district chief's car. If the fire was big enough to be classed as two-alarm, it might involve as many as thirteen vehicles; a three-alarm fire would demand even more.

❦ This communications center tracks and controls firefighting crews. The city map on the left shows where all the vehicles are. The lighted board on the right shows each vehicle's status, by color: at the station, on the way, or already at the scene of the emergency.

needed, the dispatcher alerts the fire department's own communications center, which sends out the vehicles.

This call to Fire Hall No. 15 comes first over the printer and then by voice, over the public-address system. It tells the platoon captain what's wrong and where, and which vehicles to send. In thirty or forty seconds the fire hall doors roll open and the trucks are on their way. As the pumper and two ladder trucks have all been called this time, the automatic doors roll shut on a deserted fire hall.

The pumper engine leads the way, lights flashing and siren sounding, with the ladder trucks following. Most motorists pull over to the curb and stop, as the law demands, but a few cruise blindly down the road, not noticing the lights, sirens, or airhorns. Others – incredibly – try to race the engines, or even pass them. Most pedestrians stop to stare as the trucks roll by, but there's usually somebody thoughtless enough to dash across the trucks' path. The drivers are tense as they scan the road for dangers and delays. They know that, when lives are at risk, every second counts.

"If you don't arrive in less than five minutes," says Luc Thibault, of the Montreal Fire Protection Department, "the fire will *double* every minute after that." Some fire departments use a computerized map to show them the fastest route to the fire; the map is updated every day with information about temporary road closings and road construction. Some trucks carry GPS (Global Positioning System) so they can be guided to the fire by signals from satellites.

When they pull up to the fire site, the crews find people gawking at a building with smoke seeping from the upper windows. A police car is just arriving. As the officers move bystanders out of the way, the captain sizes up the situation and calls by radio for more support. Then the captain lays out a strategy based on a few basic principles: smoke, heat, and gas always rise, if they can; the oxygen in fresh air makes a fire burn faster; fresh air and cold water will affect the way fire and smoke travel.

🔥 Fire crews have to understand the tricks that fire can play. For example, as a fire burns in one room, flammable gases rise to the ceilings of neighboring rooms. These gases get hotter and hotter. When they reach their flash point, they burst into a wall of flame that rolls across the ceiling and down the walls. This dangerous *rollover* (or *flameover*) is one reason why anyone in a fire should stay close to the floor.

The crew from the ladder truck go into action first. They're divided into an inside team and an outside team. The inside team enters the building – breaking in any way they can – to find out exactly where the fire is. That's not as easy as it sounds; because of the way smoke moves, they often have to use their training and experience to hunt it down. "You can tell when you're getting close," says veteran firefighter Frank Lawrence. "Your ears start to tingle. When they start to burn a little more, you know you're pretty much on the scene."

Once they find the fire, they use an extinguisher to put it out, if possible. They also search for anyone who needs rescuing. If it's a large fire, they may

◊ Firefighters often have to work without masks, despite the smoke and fumes, so they can see what they're doing.

FLASHOVER

A fire usually starts with one source of flame – maybe a cigarette burning on a sofa, or a frying pan of blazing oil. As the room gets hotter, though, other furnishings reach their flash point, and the whole room can burst into flame, with no warning. This dangerous moment – when a fire in a room turns into a room on fire – is called *flashover*, or *burnover*.

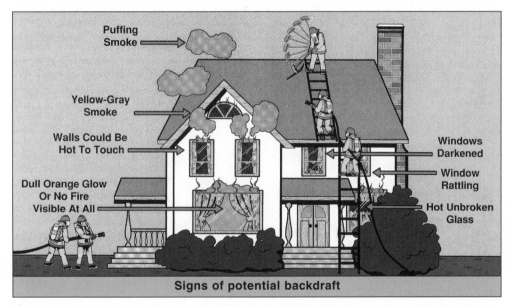

Puffing Smoke

Yellow-Gray Smoke

Walls Could Be Hot To Touch

Dull Orange Glow Or No Fire Visible At All

Windows Darkened

Window Rattling

Hot Unbroken Glass

Signs of potential backdraft

🔥 This diagram from a firefighting textbook points out the warning signs of *backdraft*. When a fire burns in a closed area, it uses up the oxygen. The flames go out, leaving a thick smoke of unburned particles, but the room remains hot enough to burn. If somebody lets in fresh air – by breaking a window or just opening a door – the new oxygen feeds the fire and it explodes in a fireball of flaming gas. This backdraft is extremely dangerous because it happens when the fire seems to have gone out, and because a fire-free area – an adjoining room or hallway – can be instantly engulfed in flames.

🔥 Firefighters huddle low for safety, waiting for their hoses to be charged so they can break into a burning home. Though this inferno looks daunting, it's more predictable than a smoldering fire in a sealed building.

have to search the whole building on their hands and knees, looking and feeling for victims. (Because heat and smoke rise, the air near the ground is cooler and less poisonous.) At this stage, everyone's most important job is to rescue people.

Meanwhile, the outside ladder team raises the aerial ladder and sends someone up to *ventilate* ("vent") the building. This means cutting a carefully placed

🔥 As a blaze demolishes a stretch of railroad freight sheds, firefighters struggle to save the building next door. Reflective strips on their clothes make them easy to spot even in smoky darkness.

hole in the roof, usually directly over the fire. Smoke and hot gas, and even flames, may shoot out when the roof is punctured. There's also the risk that the burning roof will collapse under the firefighters' weight. "You're gonna take a beating, but you just gotta keep going," says one firefighter. "There are firemen underneath you, trying to enter a room or make a burning stairway. There might be civilians. You must draw that heat and fire away from them."

❡ A pumper engine is a complex machine, and the high-pressure hoses running from it can be dangerous. Whenever water is being pumped, the driver of the engine stays at the control panel. This pumper is at the scene of a five-alarm fire in a field where old truck parts were stored, covered in highly flammable grease and wrapped in wax paper.

❡ The two big gauges at the top of the pumper's control panel show the pressure of the water coming in from the hydrant and being pumped out by the engine; the next row shows the pressure in each hose. The big black panel, middle right, has a relief valve in case there's too much pressure going into a hose; that could make the hose uncontrollable. A tube can be attached to the big hatch beside that to draw up water from a lake or pond.

Through all of this, the captain and other senior officers are keeping a close eye on how the fire is moving and growing. If they see it getting too dangerous, they'll order the crews out. One fire was so intense that it melted some of the lights on the fire truck, and even burned one of the truck's seats. A sweltering firefighter up on the aerial ladder had to be called back, for safety's sake, and hosed down with cold water. "Firefighters, they'll do pretty near anything, and you have to keep reminding them of the dangers of the job," says Commissioner Leo Stapleton of the Boston Fire Department. "They're so concentrated on trying to achieve their objective that they'll lose sight of some safety aspects."

Once the roof has been broken open to draw the fire upward, other members of the ladder company may open up doors and windows to let more air in, and to help rescue victims. They may also bring in powerful fans to control the flow of smoke and fresh air.

Venting the building lets heat, smoke, and dangerous gases escape, so the crews inside can continue their search more safely, and it also helps prevent flashover and backdraft. But the fresh supply of air makes the fire burn even more fiercely, so it has to be drenched with water as quickly as possible.

Meanwhile the engine crew is preparing the lines (hoses). A line filled with high-pressure water is a very dangerous tool. It's heavy and almost as solid as a steel pipe, and the power of the water makes it hard to hold. The lines are carefully laid in position and connected to hydrants, and water from the hydrants is pumped up to high pressure to charge the lines. As soon as the building has been vented, the engine crew open up their nozzles, driving a blast of smoke and steam through the roof and broken windows.

It usually takes two or three people to control a hose. The person at the front uses a handle to turn the water on and off, and twists the nozzle to shoot a narrow, solid stream that will reach a long way, or a wider fog or mist that will dampen and smother a larger area. People farther back help control the weight and force of the hose.

🔥 When you're handling a large hose on your own, sometimes the most practical approach is to sit on it. This stubborn blaze was in a plant that makes hardwood flooring. "We poured on tons of water, but the sawdust went on burning for hours," recalls firefighter Donna LaRush.

As the heat turns the water into steam, it can expand to 1,700 times its original volume. (One teacup of water creates over 10 cubic feet of steam — enough to fill about a fifth of a phone booth.) All this steam helps cool and smother the fire. Hoses can also be used to help vent the building; a fog of water sprayed out the window will draw out smoke and heat.

The pumper-engine crew gradually work their way into the burning building, soaking and cooling the rooms. They have to work in dense smoke and searing steam. There is the risk that the floors above will collapse onto them, or that they'll come in contact with live electrical wires. While they fight the fire from inside, the hose on the aerial-ladder apparatus is connected to

🔥 A firefighter tries desperately to reach eight crew members trapped on the upper floors of a blazing building. All eight survived the fire, but one suffered serious burns and another broke both legs. When firefighters joke about the dangers of their job, they're using humor as a way to control their fears. They know, better than anyone, how quickly a day's work can turn into disaster.

the pumper, and water is poured onto the building from above. "It's kind of like organized chaos," says firefighter Eddie Munroe. "But everybody is actually doing something, everybody is contributing in some way."

Captain Kevin Shaw remembers one day when everything was going wrong. First a hot ember fell inside his boot, burning his foot. As soon as he could reach a hose, he flooded the boot with water; but shortly after that, his foot — the burned one — broke through the charred floorboards. He managed

DEALING WITH FEELINGS

Sometimes, by the time firefighters reach the people in a burning building, it's too late to save them. Other times it's a fellow firefighter who dies. When crews work so bravely and tirelessly to save lives, it's difficult for them to accept these deaths. They try to help each other through their distress, and sometimes they have *critical incident stress debriefings*, where they can talk about their feelings and come to terms with the pain.

to tug his foot free, only to have the valve on his SCBA tank stick, cutting off his air supply. He laughs at the memory now, but it was a day that could easily have ended in tragedy.

Once the blaze seems to be more or less out, the crew work their way through the soaking black mess of the building, *overhauling* – searching for spots where the fire is still smoldering. They have to remember that the building has been weakened by the fire; there's still a risk that a wall or a floor will collapse. Cautiously they rip up floorboards, tear open mattresses, and poke holes in the ceiling, sluicing water on any remaining hot areas. They may drag charred furniture outside, and shovel out burned debris. If they have time, they may mop up the water and put tarpaulins over the holes they've cut in the roof. But whatever salvaging they do, a home that has come through a fire is a terrible sight: carpets and furniture sodden with water; plastics melted and twisted, wood charred; everything coated with greasy black soot, and reeking of smoke and gases.

Once they're satisfied that they've done as much as they can, the firefighters start the tedious job of uncoupling their hoses, draining them, and loading them on the truck. They pack up the rest of their gear and head back to the station, to wash off the filth and smoke of the fire, check out their equipment, and do their paperwork – until the alarm sounds again.

WILDFIRE!

Imagine a hot summer day in the forest. A breeze whispers in the treetops high over-head, but down below the only sound is a slight rustling as some small animal — a beetle? a chipmunk? — scurries through the parched vegetation of the forest floor.

There's a rumbling in the distance, and then another, and soon a cluster of dark clouds rolls across the sky, bringing relief from the heat. The clouds are thunderheads, carrying a strong electrical charge, and suddenly a bolt of lightning blasts through a tall old tree. The tree splits down the middle, and one half crashes to the ground. In its heart is a kernel of heat from the lightning — and that small, smoldering kernel lands on a bed of paper-dry leaves, twigs, and pine needles. . . .

Wildland fires are terrible to watch. They sweep away huge tracts of beautiful woods, and many of the animals that live there. But some of these fires are part of a natural process. They clear away the choking tangle of old, diseased trees and brush, and make room for healthy new growth. Some trees actually depend on forest fires. The jack pine needs the fire's heat to release seeds from its pine cones, and the Douglas fir grows well only in the open spaces left by fire. Often, when a fire is spotted, forest officials decide that it's best to keep a close eye on it but to let it burn naturally, until it burns itself out. But some fires are dangerous to people in the area, or threaten to do too much damage.

How much damage is too much?

Year by year we encroach more and more on nature, putting up homes, resorts, and other facilities in or near woodlands. We also use our forests as a source of commercial timber. When wildfire breaks out, wildland firefighters are called on to protect these valuable assets.

THE FIRES OF '98

In 1998, firefighters were called in from all over the United States to battle wildfires in northern Florida. Half a million acres of forest burned away, and over three hundred homes and businesses were damaged or destroyed. The interstate highway was closed for days, and smoke cut off Florida's sunlight all the way south to Miami, 250 miles (400 km) away. When the Fourth of July rolled around, the traditional fireworks were banned, for fear of starting even more blazes. Most years, the residents of the "sunshine state" fear tropical rainstorms and hurricanes; in 1998, many people were praying for one.

And while some fire is a healthy part of forest regeneration, too much wildfire is wasteful and destructive. In wiping out a forest, a fire may also do long-lasting damage to the forest floor. A carelessly discarded cigarette, a poorly extinguished campfire – and vast areas of healthy woods can go up in flames. When the weather is dry enough, even a small spark from a machine may be enough to start a fire. Millions of acres of forest are burned every year, and much of the destruction is caused by people.

Fire turns the tables

When a fire starts in a city or town, firefighters can usually surround the blaze, and tap into a piped water supply. If necessary, they can bring in extra trucks and gear from nearby towns and cities. They can send injured crew members to hospital, and call up fresh teams to replace them.

In a wildland fire it's the other way around: the firefighters are the ones who are surrounded. They can never be sure where the blaze will head next, or how large it will grow. Big fires can jump across roads, swamps, even lakes. They can become firestorms — blazes so powerful that they create their own weather systems. If the wind suddenly changes direction, a hill or valley that seemed like a safe retreat can become an inferno. Wildland firefighters often work without piped water and make do without trucks and other heavy equipment. Backup — even rescue — may be hours away.

Because forest fires can be so large, many volunteer firefighters work alongside the professionals. With hundreds of people attacking the fire from the ground and from the air, planning and coordination are

♨ Observers living in lofty fire towers in remote forest areas keep a sharp eye out for signs of fire. As well, lightning strikes can be tracked by computer, so that planes can later fly over the region and check for smoke. The heat of a lightning strike can be over 60,000°F (33,300°C).

essential. Crews at the fire scene report their findings by radio. The fire is tracked from airplanes, both by sight and by thermal imagery. It may even be

🔥 *Hot-shots* – professional firefighters trained to work on large or small wildfires – pause to review their plans. Many hot-shots are former smokejumpers, experienced in parachuting into fire areas.

A BIRD'S-EYE VIEW

One of the newest and most sophisticated tools against wildland fire is AVIRIS (Airborne Visible and Infra-Red Imaging Spectrometer), developed for the American space agency, NASA. From an aircraft flying 12 miles (19 km) above sea level, at 450 miles (720 km) an hour, AVIRIS can examine a forest, measuring molecules of chlorophyll, water, and cellulose. These measurements can be used to calculate what plants are in the area, and how dry they are. This information can be vital. In 1994, a fire on Colorado's Storm King Mountain moved into a forest of Gambel oak – a tree that gets extremely flammable when it's dry. Fire crews were suddenly trapped by flames the height of a ten-story building. Fourteen firefighters died.

tracked from space, by satellites, using GPS (Global Positioning System). Computers translate all this information into an ever-changing map of the fire's progress.

On the ground, crews race to cut off the fire's fuel by creating *firelines* — cutting down trees, burning away strips of vegetation, digging trenches down to rock or bare soil. If they're lucky, they may be able to bring in bulldozers and chain saws for this heavy labor. If not, it will all be done by hand.

Sometimes crews use *drip torches*, which leave a trail of burning diesel and gas fuel, to set their own fires; the idea is to starve the forest fire by burning up its fuel before it gets there. If they can't get close enough to use drip torches, they may use flare guns to shoot incendiary flares into the target area.

Attack from the air

While ground crews slave away on the fireline, airplanes and helicopters can carry out a host of jobs above them. They can airlift pumps, miles of hose, and

🔥 This Canadair CL-415 is a *water bomber*, built especially for fighting fires. It has both floats and wheels, so it can land either on the ground or on water. Tanks in its hull hold about 1,400 gallons (6,000 l) of water and firefighting foam. By skimming over the surface of a lake at high speed for just twelve seconds, the plane can suck up enough water to refill its tanks; then it's ready to head back to the fire.

other equipment to where it's needed. Observers can fly around the fire, warning the fire crews of its speed and direction. If ground crews can't get close enough to set their own fires, to burn up the fuel, *aerial ignition devices* — little balls filled with incendiary chemicals — may be dropped from a helicopter to set the chosen patch ablaze.

If water is needed, a helicopter may airlift a *bucket* — a scoop that hangs below the helicopter and holds about 400 gallons (1,500 l). Some helicopters even have built-in water tanks. The water can be offloaded directly on the fire, or dumped in a tank to supply the fire crews' hoses. There are also planes that can scoop up water from nearby lakes, and dump it on the fire or on endangered woods nearby. Planes can blanket the woods with *slurry*, a fire retardant, to cut off the fire's oxygen supply.

🔥 Smokejumpers – parachuting firefighters – prepare for their jump. The masks on their helmets will protect their faces if they have to drop down through the trees.

🔥 The white section under this Bell 205 helicopter is a *belly tank* that holds 300 gallons (1,200 l) of water. The pilot fills the tank by hovering over a lake and dropping a suction hose.

When a fire in the depths of the forest is still fairly small, professional firefighters known as *smokejumpers* may parachute down near the fire zone from an airplane. First the pilot and a spotter pick out the target area; then they drop streamers to see how the winds are blowing. If conditions are safe for jumping, the smokejumpers go in, circling the area as they glide down, looking for the best place to land. If the forest is dense, they may have to *thread the needle* – parachute right down among the trees. If they are falling too fast, they may have to slow their descent by doing a *tree jump* – purposely landing in the treetops, so the parachute snags in the branches, and then lowering themselves by rope. It's a daring feat; a small miscalculation can mean broken bones.

Once they land, smokejumpers collect their heavy equipment, which is sent down to them by parachute, and set off for the fire. Their backpacks may weigh as much as 110 pounds (50 kg) – so much that it's hard to stand up without help. When they finish the job of putting out the fire, usually by laborious digging and shoveling, they may have to carry those heavy backpacks many miles across rough country.

Another way to get in is by *rap attack*: rappeling down a rope from a helicopter 200 to 300 feet (60 to 90 m) off the ground. Rappelers wear a special body harness that lets them control how fast they slide down the rope. A rap attack team usually has five members: the pilot, a spotter, and three rappelers. Like the smokejumpers, they begin with a *recce* (reconnaissance, or look around), circling the region by air to check wind conditions, the slope of the land, and the best way in. Heavy equipment like pumps and saws can be lowered to them by rope. Since they're wearing helmets, they often hang their hard hats on bands on their legs. As well, since they need their hands free for rappeling, they may clip their bags of gear to their harnesses.

Candles, crowns, and canopies

Sometimes fire creeps through the underbrush, burning at ground level and *candling* or *torching* – shooting up trees one by one. It can roar across the

🔥 How does it feel to rappel down a rope into a fire zone? Johanna Gunn explains: "We do over one hundred rappels from a practice tower before we first go from a helicopter, and after that we keep doing proficiencies – five practice rappels off a tower every seven days. So it becomes pretty much second nature. But it's still very exciting."

forest floor – downhill or uphill – as fast as 30 miles (48 km) an hour. Other times the fire moves by *crowning*: it races through the forest canopy by hopping from one blazing treetop to another, high above the firefighters' heads. Fire can even spread underground, burning away the roots of trees so they collapse without warning.

But the fire itself is not the only danger. Temperatures of up to 2,000°F (over 1,000°C) turn the forest into a deadly bowling alley. As charred trees topple and roots are consumed by flames, boulders come tumbling down the hills. *Snags* – blazing branches – crash to the ground and roll downhill. However busy and weary the fire crews are, they have to be constantly alert.

❧ As a ground fire reaches the base of these trees, it torches up to set the whole tree ablaze.

🔥 Wildfire crews carry one item they hope they'll never, ever have to use – the fire shelter. It's a small tent of aluminum foil (to reflect the heat away) and fiberglass. Somebody who is trapped by the fire, with no way out, can lie tucked under the tent and try to hang on while the fire and smoke pass by. "We call them 'shake and bake' because it looks like something you'd wrap a potato in before you stuck it in the oven," says a firefighter who has used his tent only once in nine years. "The fire shelter is the absolute last resort."

Because the winds change often, and unpredictably, smoke is another major hazard. "You eat a lot of smoke, and you can't get out of it," says smokejumper Doug Houston. "You end up going to your knees, and you feel like you can't breathe. You try to run out of it, but there's no place to go."

Fire crews may work as long as thirty-six or forty hours before they can snatch a few hours of rest in a sleeping bag. If they're lucky enough to be near a base camp, they'll get a real meal as well. If not, they'll make do with emergency rations. Most of the food is canned so it won't be spoiled by the fumes.

THE RACE THAT COULDN'T BE WON

One of the worst wildland-fire disasters was in Montana, in 1949. Foreman Wagner Dodge and his team of smokejumpers were suddenly trapped by fire in a valley called Mann Gulch. The only way out was up over the top of a steep ridge, but that was half a mile, and – unlike people – fire actually travels faster uphill. The crew abandoned their heavy tools and ran for safety, but the fire moved even more swiftly, and soon it was only 50 yards (meters) behind them. In a desperately bold move, Dodge decided to stop and build a small fire in the path of the blaze. His *escape fire* quickly burned away the brush, and he ordered his men to throw themselves onto the bare, smoldering ground in the hope that the main fire would pass them by. It was a daring move, and too bizarre for the others. They refused and kept running for safety. Dodge survived by hugging the scorched soil as the fuel-hungry fire roared past him, bringing winds so strong that several times he was lifted right off the ground. Two men reached safety at the top of the ridge. The other thirteen died.

"About all you have is a spoon and a can opener," says rap-attacker Johanna Gunn. "People take refried beans and stewed tomatoes and tinned corn, and mush them all together, and eat them cold. It sounds weird, but after a long hard day it tastes pretty good."

When a fire seems to be out, there's still a lot of work to do. Teams have to trek through the ruins, searching and sniffing for wisps of smoke, raking open hot spots and dousing them with water. *Smudges* – patches of underground fire – have to be dug up and extinguished. Even one smoldering root or branch could be enough to start another fire.

🔥 A burned-out forest is a grim sight, but in a few years this woodland will be green again.

Fighting wildfire is a filthy, back-breaking, dangerous job – yet many of the people who do it find it irresistible. "It gets addicting," says smokejumper Mike Stebbing. "It gets in your blood, and it can be fun, and that's why we're here."

SHIPS, PLANES, AND SUBWAY TRAINS

"The back motors of the [airship Hindenburg*] are holding it just enough to keep it —
It's burst into flame! Get out of the way! . . . get out of the way, please! It is bursting
into flames. This is terrible! This is one of the worst catastrophes in the world! The flames
are 500 feet into the sky. It is a terrific crash, ladies and gentlemen. It is in smoke and
flames now. Oh, the humanity! Those passengers! I can't talk. . . ."*

– Radio reporter Herb Morrison

In May 1937 the *Hindenburg* was arriving in the United States from
Germany. Held aloft by a framework filled with gasbags, the airship had
luxurious private sleeping-berths and elegant public rooms. But there was
an ominous touch to the smoking-room: the cigarette lighter was chained in
place. A steward carried matches to light pipes and cigars, but passengers were
strictly forbidden to carry matches anywhere on board. For the gasbags keeping this "floating palace" in the sky were filled with hydrogen, a highly
flammable gas. When the ship burst into a fireball 25 yards (meters) above the
ground — perhaps from a hydrogen leak, or perhaps through deliberate sabo-
tage — thirty-six people lost their lives.

Travel brings us knowledge, pleasure, and convenience, but sometimes it also brings danger. We may be moving at high speed, or confined to a small space, or distanced from the security of solid land and open air. A ship may be driven by flammable fuel, or nuclear propulsion; a fire in the narrow nooks and corridors below decks is difficult to fight, and if the fire gets out of control there's no place to escape to except the water. Rail and subway trains are often packed with rush-hour crowds, and may be caught in the dark of underground tunnels. And what could be more frightening than a fire in space – like the 1997 blaze on the Soviet space station *Mir*, when an oxygen tank burst into flames that fire extinguishers couldn't put out?

Special dangers like these call for special precautions. Fortunately, these days we know a lot about fire prevention, and we have organizations that set strict safety rules. Not so fortunately, people still tend to be thoughtless about the risk of fire. When a blaze claims lives in a vessel or vehicle, it's often because somebody tried to save time, trouble, or money by ignoring the rules.

The Tragedy of the SS Noronic

About six p.m. on a Friday in September 1949, the passenger ship *Noronic* docked in Toronto. The ship had come from Detroit, and was due to set out next morning on a scenic cruise through the Thousand Islands. It was carrying 524 passengers, mostly American and Canadian, and 171 crew, many of whom were not on duty that night.

Around 2:30 in the morning, a passenger noticed smoke coming from a supply locker, and alerted a crew member. The two tried to put out the fire with an extinguisher, but the blaze was too large. They tried to use a fire hose, but no water came out. The passenger ran to get his family off the ship, but he didn't tell other passengers. The crewman rang a fire alarm in the social hall, but the bell wasn't loud enough to awaken most people. Nobody went to warn them. There was no automatic alarm system.

The *Noronic* was exempt from many regulations about ship construction, for various reasons. As a result, much of the vessel was built of wood, and decorated in flammable materials like canvas and masonite. With no sprinkler system,

🔥 A fireboat tries to douse the dreadful blaze on the *Noronic*. Badly trained crew, malfunctioning equipment, flammable materials, and inadequate escape routes – factors like these have played a role in many ship disasters over the years.

there was nothing to stop the flames.

When the first mate (a senior officer) learned of the fire, he tried to call for help by sounding the ship's klaxon. It malfunctioned, and the signal wasn't heard. By the time a watchman on shore spotted the flames and called the fire department, the blaze had spread across the ship.

Firefighters arrived to find the top three decks ablaze, with passengers screaming for help, and some leaping into the cold waters of Lake Ontario. Crews set to work quickly, laying hose from hydrants, setting up a suction hose into the lake, and extending the aerial trucks' wooden ladders from shore to ship. A fireboat got close enough to dump water into the burning bow, and a rescue squad began hauling survivors up from the darkness of the lake, using ropes and ladders. But many people awoke too late to escape from their cabins. Others got as far as the deck and then found their path blocked; renovations of the ship's original design had left them no direct gangway to the pier. Some who did reach the deck lost track of which side of the ship they were on; trying to jump into the lake, they fell to their deaths on the pavement of the pier. The crew members got themselves to safety, but 118 passengers died.

In 1904 – forty-five years before the *Noronic* tragedy – the steamboat *General Slocum* was sailing up New York's East River, heading for a Sunday School picnic, when a boy warned the captain that he'd seen smoke. For some reason the captain ignored the warning. Even when police and firefighters spotted the smoke from shore and came out by boat to help, he continued up the river, expecting his crew to put out the fire, instead of getting passengers off the boat. But the crew hardly knew what to do; they had never even had a fire drill. When they managed to dig out a fire hose and some life preservers, both were so old and rotten that they fell to pieces. Despite desperate rescue efforts from shore, 1,030 people died – and every one of them could have been saved.

Today we have strict rules to try to prevent disasters like these. Ships have to be built in certain ways with certain kinds of materials, just as buildings do. There are rules about how many passengers a boat can hold. There has to be a life jacket for every passenger, and large boats need life rafts as well. There are rules about how much firefighting and rescue equipment has to be on board, how well it has to be maintained, and how often it has to be inspected. Commercial ships have crew members specially trained for fires and other emergencies, and regular fire drills are held so the whole crew knows exactly how to deal with trouble. Yet inspectors find that many people still try to cheat on the rules, gambling – like the owners and crew of the *Noronic* and the *General Slocum* – that a fire won't happen.

🔥 Waterfronts pose special fire risks. They are often lined with wooden docks and warehouses, and the wood may be soaked with creosote (a flammable, tarry material) to keep it from rotting. The warehouses may contain dangerous materials that change week by week, as one cargo arrives and another leaves, and there may be giant fuel-storage tanks as well. Boats moored along the pier hold tanks of fuel and propane gas. And if a fire does start, fire trucks may not be able to reach it.

To deal with these problems, waterfront cities often use fireboats – like the *William Lyon Mackenzie*, shown fighting a massive blaze on a freighter in Toronto harbor. Fireboats have powerful pumps to suck up water and stream it far into the flames. When they're close enough to land, they can also pump up water to supply the fire engines. If possible, a burning boat will be set adrift, or even towed away from shore, so the blaze doesn't spread. (The trouble with pumping water onto a boat fire is that all that extra weight may sink the boat!)

Aviation fires

Fire is a pilot's nightmare. High in the sky, boxed into a cramped machine with many unreachable areas, crew and passengers are surrounded by tanks of fuel that can burst into fireballs, as well as high-pressure oxygen tanks, and a host of flammable chemicals and materials in the cabin, the plane's structure, and even the cargo.

Over the years the aircraft industry has worked to improve fire safety, and there are now elaborate measures to prevent and put out fires. Planes loaded with cameras, electronic sensors, and test dummies have been crashed on purpose, so researchers could study what happened and how real-life passengers could have been protected. The larger and more expensive the plane is, the more sophisticated the fire precautions can be.

There are smoke detectors throughout most large commercial planes. There may be heat sensors in the toilets, and sprinklers in the cabin. Crews learn to use portable extinguishers for cabin fires. Places that can't be reached in flight – such as fuel tanks inside the wings, and some cargo areas – can be flooded with a gas that puts out the fire but doesn't conduct electricity or leave a mess behind. Interior fabrics are treated to resist fire. Although the crash of a plane can create a spectacular fireball, it's usually from highly flammable fuel vapor, which burns at a relatively low temperature. Treated fabrics can often resist the blaze long enough to let passengers escape to safety.

RED OR **YELLOW, YELLOW** OR RED . . .

Though fire trucks are traditionally red, yellow is more visible at night. On the other hand, absent-minded motorists are more likely to think, "Oh-oh, a fire truck!" if they see red. While city fire departments mull over this decision – some switching to yellow, others staying with red – chromium yellow is the international standard for airports.

🔥 Because airport fire engines like these have to rush straight to the fire, they are often *all-terrain vehicles*, with enormous tires, crash bars, and high, reinforced fronts. If there's a fence in their path, they'll go right through it; they just don't have time to go around. So that a small crew can mobilize as many trucks as possible, most airport fire vehicles are designed to be operated by one person, so the steering wheel is sometimes in the middle of the cab, rather than on the left.

If the plane has to make an emergency landing, track lighting illuminates the floor, leading passengers to the exits even in heavy smoke. (The lighting is white down the aisles, and red at the exits.) There are many emergency exits, at doors and windows, and some have slides or chutes to help people reach the ground. If the plane can get to a major airport, chromium-yellow emergency trucks will be standing by when it lands.

Small crews, big emergencies

A blazing airplane is a huge emergency that calls for a massive response. Fortunately, though, blazing airplanes are extremely rare, and it's obviously not practical to keep a hundred firefighters at the airport just in case a plane catches fire sometime this year. How can a small crew deal with a crisis of this size?

The first answer is *speed* – they have to get there fast and act fast. When an emergency call comes in, airport crews don't wait for details; they get their trucks rolling, and hear the rest over the radio. First to arrive are usually the *rapid-intervention vehicles*, small foam pumpers built for speed. They're followed by bigger foam pumpers that have tall turrets to shoot foam higher and farther, and *ground-sweep* nozzles to lay down a layer of foam. Some pumpers have infrared cameras on the roof, so they can find the plane quickly through darkness and smoke.

The pumpers have enough foam to last two or three minutes, and they can spray the foam about 75 yards (meters). Some have *piercing nozzles* so they can punch a hole right through the airplane's fuselage and pump water-mist or foam inside. The trucks can also pump dry chemicals, and they may have Class D extinguishers for flammable materials like titanium, a strong, light-weight metal used in airplane construction. As well, they carry a range of rescue and first-aid equipment.

The second answer for a small crew facing a big emergency is *focus* – that is, concentrating on creating a rescue/escape corridor for people inside. Wherever passengers and crew are getting out of the plane, firefighters try to hold back the flames. Foam and water can be used to protect the fuselage, and

🔥 The wreckage of this DC-3 lies blanketed with foam. Note that the firefighter in the center is still wearing an aluminized heat hood. Airport vehicles carry some ladders and water hoses, but their main firefighting job is dealing with burning *hydrocarbons* like oil and fuel. If there's a building fire (in the air terminal, for example) they may ask for help from nearby city fire halls. Likewise, if city crews have a major hydrocarbon fire (perhaps in an oil tank), they may ask the airport team to send foam pumpers.

to push back pools of flaming fuel. "We take our cue from the flight crew, when we can," says Deputy Chief Bill Ives. "As long as people are coming out, we try to keep a fire-free area around the exits. But if they stop coming out, we're going to go in and have a look."

Going in can be harder than it sounds. If the doors are jammed, firefighters may have to cut openings in the fuselage. Letting fresh air into the fire creates the risk of flashover. In their heavy protective gear, loaded with tools and other equipment, they may have trouble climbing into the plane. Once inside, they face narrow aisles jammed with luggage and debris. But they have be sure the plane is empty – and perhaps bring out injured or disabled passengers – before they can focus on extinguishing the fire.

When they finally head back to the fire hall to clean up, it doesn't mean they're through. They'll be on hand as the fuel-soaked wreckage is carefully examined and removed, over weeks or months, in case a spark sets off another fire. They'll also take part in the investigation, which may go on for a year or more.

"Learn or burn"

If ships and airplanes both pose fire hazards, imagine a combination of the two. On a modern aircraft carrier, pilots land fighter planes on deck with only a narrow safety margin, while the ship itself tosses in the sea. The carrier may hold huge amounts of jet fuel, as well as ammunition, missiles, and bombs. Firefighting is complicated by the dangerous suction and exhaust streams of jet engines, and by the whirling rotor blades of helicopters, and the gusts of wind and charges of static electricity they create.

In 1967 a mishandled rocket exploded on the deck of the American aircraft carrier USS *Forestall*. The explosion set off a chain reaction that killed most of the crash-and-rescue team, and the fire burned out of control for two days. In all, 134 crew members died. It was a grim reminder that on ships – especially warships – there is no room for carelessness; crew are warned, "The rules are written in blood." The navy's fire safety instructors put it even more succinctly: "Learn or burn."

Trains above ground

Like buildings, railway trains that carry passengers often have smoke detectors and public-address systems, and crews are trained to deal with emergencies. When something goes wrong on a train, though, often the first sign is on the outside, down where the wheels are racing over the tracks. To catch the problem early, detectors underneath the cars can monitor changes and pass information to a computerized *black box*; any sign of trouble is instantly transmitted to the engineer and the dispatch office. There may even be *hotbox detectors* along the track system, checking each car of every passing train for overheating and other problems.

Trains below ground

At King's Cross, in London, England, a below-ground maze of ticket halls, tunnels, stairways, escalators, and elevators connects two railway lines and five busy Underground (subway) lines. At 7:29 p.m. on a work day in November 1987, a passenger told a ticket clerk that some garbage near the top of one of the wooden escalators seemed to be on fire. The clerk reported this to the station inspector, but accidentally gave the wrong location. Warned again by another passenger, the clerk leaned out of his booth but decided it didn't look very serious. There still wasn't much smoke, and many passengers heard rumors of the fire but went up the escalator anyway.

At 7:32, the Underground police learned of the fire and called the fire department. Crews from the nearest fire station were away on another call — a false alarm, as it turned out — so crews had to be summoned from more distant stations. Delayed by traffic, they began arriving at 7:42. While they were setting up their equipment, one firefighter went down to the platform, to warn people arriving at the station not to get off the trains.

At first people waited calmly on the platforms. But then it was decided that King's Cross should be evacuated, and drivers were told not to stop their trains in the station. As the smoke grew worse and the trains rolled right by, people panicked and started fighting their way up the escalator. By now flames were licking the wooden steps; the smoke was thick and the air was getting too hot to breathe.

At 7:45 — just three minutes after the first fire engine arrived — the booking hall at the top of the escalators reached the point of flashover. A fireball swept through the hall, putting out the electric lights and setting passengers on fire. "At first there was a noise like a blast furnace," said one survivor, "then flames ripped across the ceiling as if they had been shot from a flamethrower. Then there was the choking smoke, so black and thick it seemed you could grab it by the handful." Blinded and terrified, people stumbled in the darkness, gasping for breath.

Fire crews struggled to get through the searing heat and smoke, tripping over bodies and debris, but they could barely reach the fire before their air tanks ran low and they had to turn back. Despite the heroic efforts of firefighters, police, and many civilians, thirty-one people died, including one fireman, and many more were terribly injured.

What caused such a nightmare? The fire was probably started by a discarded cigarette, but it was fed by garbage and grease that hadn't been cleaned from under the escalator. Staff of the Underground had little or no emergency training, and had no plan for evacuating people. Some of the exit gates were locked. Firefighters didn't have a detailed map of the station, and when they finally laid hands on one, it was incomplete. A hydrant, hoses, and other equipment were located only steps from where the blaze started, but they were hidden behind construction hoardings; if the first firefighters on the scene had been able to use them, the fire might never have reached flashover. Once again, people suffered and died because of thoughtless acts and careless oversights.

Fire safety underground

How do we protect people against fire when they're riding high-speed trains through underground tunnels? Most subway trains are equipped with fire extinguishers, smoke detectors, and fire alarms. The stations have all of these, and sprinkler systems as well. Many stations have special *access shafts* to let fire crews reach the train tunnel directly, without going through the station, which might be full of smoke. Some tunnels have *dry drops*, empty standpipes reaching up to the street, so water can be pumped down. Some subway systems have *portal doors* to seal off smoky tunnels, and ventilation fans to push out smoke and suck in fresh air.

People tend to panic in any fire. When they're in a dark, smoky tunnel, it's even harder to stay calm and act sensibly. Subway employees need lots of planning and practice so they can direct passengers to safety in a crisis. As for firefighters, they study the construction and layout of subway systems, and learn how to cut electric power on the lines, and how to move safely through tunnels and across live electrical rails. Some fire departments even have mock subway stations, with tunnels and tracks that can be flooded with smoke, so crews can get used to the feel of a subway fire.

VIRTUAL OIL RIGS

In 1988, flames swept through an oil rig off Scotland, and 167 people died as the structure collapsed into the icy waters of the North Sea. An inquiry into the disaster concluded that the oil rig crew had not been well enough trained. But how do you simulate a fire on something as complex and precarious as an oil rig? The answer lies in computer simulation. Control-room operators can now train in a make-believe rig on shore, with gauges and controls that imitate a real emergency. To teach students to resist panic, the room can be shaken and jolted to suggest winds, explosions, and collisions. Lights flicker and alarms sound, and the room even overheats as it would in a raging fire. It's valuable training, but students may never enjoy an amusement park again!

Special materials, special problems

The problems of a fire vary, depending on exactly what's burning. Some materials (the rubber of discarded auto tires, for example) are hard to extinguish, and give off huge quantities of thick, stinking smoke. Others – fuels, or powdery materials like sawdust – create a risk of explosion. That's why firefighters need to know what materials are stored in a burning building.

Alcohol and hydrogen fires pose yet another problem: the flames are so clear that they're almost invisible in daylight. Until recently, firefighters located these fires using the *broom method* – waving a lightweight broom ahead of them, and watching to see where the broom caught fire. But since hydrogen is used as a rocket fuel, space-age technology is now replacing the old broom. A new *fire imager*, used like a pair of binoculars, lets crews see those invisible flames from a safer distance. Fire imagers can also be used like thermal imaging cameras, to see the layout of a burning building, or to look for smoldering hot spots.

The mother of all fires

When we tap into the earth's oil supplies to get products like fuel oil and gasoline, there's always a chance that the escaping oil and natural gas will catch fire. Over the years, oil-fire specialists have become expert at capping these fires. But in 1991 they faced a challenge beyond anything they'd ever encountered.

As Iraqi troops retreated from Kuwait during the Gulf War, they deliberately set fire to Kuwait's oil wells. Valuable oil and natural gas burned away, and choking clouds of smoke blanketed the country, turning day into night. Teams of oil-fire experts from ten countries, including Canada and the United States, were called in. There were more than seven hundred fires to be put out, and some experts predicted that the job would take five years. The damage to the environment would be immeasurable.

The fires were so hot that steel equipment not only melted but vaporized, and the blaze was so thunderous – "the loudest noise you'll ever hear," said one firefighter – that crews had to communicate by hand signals. They carried metal shields as they approached the wells, to ward off the blistering heat. To protect themselves and their equipment, they reversed the oil pipelines, and used them to pump in cooling water from the Persian Gulf. Because the oil and gas were shooting out of the earth at high pressure, neither water nor foam could put out the blaze; instead, crews laid dynamite charges. The dynamite blast starved the fire of oxygen, and the blaze was snuffed out. In only nine

The firefighting in Kuwait was incredibly hot, filthy, dangerous work; sometimes oil seemed to rain from the sky, and the gases in the air were so explosive that even a spark of static electricity (from two things rubbing together, for example) might set off an explosion. Once the fire was out and the well was cool, the crew had to cap the gushing well with this metal derrick (like a giant tap). "It was like hell on earth," said firefighter Paul-Émile Ouellette.

months the hundreds of fires were extinguished, and the skies over Kuwait began to clear.

It seems the cycle never ends. We find more and more ways to use fire, but at the same time we put ourselves in more and more perilous situations. Wherever we go, in our high-tech, space-age world, we take this age-old friend and enemy along with us.

PLAYING WITH FIRE

"I have to hunt. I have to search. There's always a step, step, step. I am organized. A 'perfectionist' is what many people call me, but I don't think so. I am relentless, because the way I looked at it every patient was mine. Every fire I went to was mine. Every apartment, every room was mine. I take possession whether with a microscope, or a nozzle, or with authority as a fire marshal. . . . This is my domain and I want to do this right."

– Jack Carney, retired fire investigator

Most of us find a strange fascination in disasters. Fires, floods, explosions, earthquakes – we know they can be terribly destructive, we know they cause dreadful pain and misery, yet we can't resist looking at the news photos, watching the TV reports. Maybe we feel selfishly relieved that this horror has befallen somebody else, and not us. Maybe we are awed by the sheer power of destruction. Whatever the reason, we are often drawn to disaster, even if we feel a little ashamed of our curiosity.

Unfortunately, some people do more than watch. They commit *arson* – that is, they deliberately start fires. (*Ardeo* is Latin for "I burn"; "ardor," meaning

🔥 Investigators Donald Wundelich and Charles Frederickson interview a man who witnessed a fire. Arsonists are caught in all kinds of ways: through the pattern of their crimes, through their own suspicious behavior, and – more and more – through scientific evidence.

99

hot emotion, comes from the same root.) Arsonists are well aware that property — perhaps huge tracts of town or forest — may be destroyed. They know that innocent residents or passersby may suffer and even die. They know that firefighters will risk their lives to control the blaze and search for victims. So why do they do it?

Arson for profit

Sometimes the motive is simply money. Business isn't going well; the warehouse is full of merchandise that nobody wants to buy, and creditors are demanding payment. If the merchandise "accidentally" burns up, the insurance company will have to pay hard cash for all those unsalable products. (Some owners plan this insurance fraud from the beginning. They fill a warehouse with cheap materials such as old clothes or furnishings; then they insure them as expensive new ones, arrange a fire, and collect a large insurance payment.)

Sometimes, the aim is simply to get rid of the building. Maybe burning it is cheaper than having it safely demolished, or maybe the building has historical importance and can't legally be destroyed.

WHO PAYS FOR INSURANCE FRAUD?

Some people pretend it's all right to cheat big insurance companies because they have "deep pockets" — that is, lots of money. But insurance companies collect money from all their customers, to pay off the few who file claims. The more they pay out in claims, the more they charge their customers. Suppose the owners of bicycle stores and ice-cream shops have to pay more for insurance; that means they have to charge more for bicycles and ice cream. So who do *you* think pays for insurance fraud?

Incidental arson

Sometimes arson is used as a tool. An arsonist may set a fire to get even with an enemy, or to drive a rival out of business. Criminal organizations threaten arson to extort money from businesses; those that don't pay may have a visit from a *torch* (a professional arsonist). Someone who has committed another crime may start a fire to try to burn up documents and destroy fingerprints and other evidence. Fire may be a weapon of hatred – against another race or religion, for example – or an attack on society, as in a riot or rebellion.

Whatever the reason for arson, it is a reckless, dangerous crime. Fire can be a swift and unpredictable force. Once it's been unleashed, there is no telling what damage will be done, or who will suffer. More than seven hundred people are killed by arson every year in the United States alone. Often, the arsonist is the first to die in the flames.

Kids who set fires

For some fire-setters, the fire itself is reason enough. Small children may be drawn to this forbidden danger by curiosity, perhaps inventing fantasies about fire, not understanding what they are risking. Older children who feel confused and powerless may try to express their resentment and insecurity, or to get attention, by starting fires. *Many of the children who die in fires started the fires themselves*, for one reason or another. Unfortunately, families sometimes keep quiet about this behavior. If someone you know has set a fire, or seems interested in setting fires, don't keep it a secret. Tell an adult, or call your local fire department. Firefighters spend a lot of time teaching safety and prevention, and some fire departments offer counseling for fire-setting kids, and run special activity programs to help them understand the dangers and control their curiosity.

Arson as a disease

Adults who set fires for no apparent reason are called *firebugs* or *pyromaniacs*. They may set a lot of small fires, as many as ten or twenty in an hour. Some

FIRE BUFFS

People who are fascinated by fires and firefighting may spend their spare time at the fire hall, helping to take care of the equipment; they may become volunteer or even full-time firefighters. They may show up at fire scenes, take pictures, collect books and souvenirs. All this is fine, and often very helpful. But fascinations can get out of hand. Once in a while it turns out that a "fire buff" – maybe a volunteer who helps around the fire hall, maybe even someone praised as a fire hero – was actually the person who started the blaze. The magic of fire has a dark side – and sometimes the dark side wins.

choose places where they think the fires won't do serious harm, while others show no concern for the damage they may do.

One man with a long history of fire-setting tried to describe his feelings:

Yes, I knew that I might take human lives – but I want to tell you about how I felt. I just couldn't help setting fires – just like I can't help stealing things. I never started one fire without hoping it wouldn't be bad, and that it wouldn't cause injury or death; but I knew it might. . . . I'm a criminal and I know it.

Firebugs tend to be people with other serious problems in life: unhappy relationships, unsuccessful careers. Many are heavy drinkers. It's not clear why they turn to arson, or what they get out of it. But whatever their problems, whatever their fire-setting patterns, pyromaniacs are mentally disturbed. They are a grave danger to themselves and to others.

Catching firebugs

The business of detecting arson begins while the fire is still burning.

FALSE ALARMS

Some people wouldn't dream of setting a fire on purpose, but think it's harmless fun to set off a fire alarm and watch the engines arrive. The trouble is that, in a real fire, even a small delay can kill people — and firefighters rushing to a phony call may not get to a real call in time. Remember the fire in King's Cross station? Fire engines spent ten minutes fighting their way through traffic, and thirty-one people died. How many might have lived if the nearest fire crews hadn't been wasting their time on a false alarm?

 Firefighters don't just extinguish the blaze; they also look for where the fire started, and how. They check whether doors and windows are locked, and look for signs of explosive or *incendiary* (fire-starting) devices. They notice who's standing around, enjoying the spectacle – and who's quietly sneaking away.

Firefighters check the weather and wind, and watch to see if the fire grows too quickly, or in an unexpected direction. They watch for suspicious smells, and flame or smoke of an unusual color. Any of these signs could mean that some-one has doused the property with an *accelerant* – something highly flammable, like gasoline – to make it burn more readily.

Once the fire is extinguished, they examine the house inside and out. Signs of a break-in, such as a forced lock, may point to arson, as may other signs of tampering. Even something as basic as broken window-glass can hold all kinds of clues. If splinters far away from the fire are clean, the fire may have started with an explosion; if the splinters are closer, and smoky, the explosion was more likely caused by the fire. Broken glass inside the building could come from an arsonist (or firefighter) breaking in; if there are splinters both inside and out, the window probably collapsed in the fire. Patterns of smoke and crazing (small cracks) suggest how hot the fire was, and how quickly it grew.

If the scene looks suspicious – or if someone has died, or the damage is very expensive – investigators are called in to comb the wreckage for evidence. They talk to witnesses about how the fire looked, sounded, and smelled. They exam-ine the *fire cone* – the V-pattern of burn marks on walls, floors, and ceilings, which usually spreads upward from wherever the fire started. They measure the depth of charring in different areas. They work with hand tools like brushes, rakes, and tweezers, but they may call in cranes and bulldozers to take the ruins apart so nothing is overlooked. They search for evidence (such as the remain-der of a gasoline can) to suggest that an accelerant or explosive was used. They make sketches, take photographs, collect samples of everything from ashes to carpets to soil, and write endless notes.

Sometimes a specially trained dog – an *accelerant-detecting canine* – is brought in to sniff out suspicious substances. The dog is led through the ruins by a han-dler, and *alerts* when it smells an accelerant – by barking, digging, or just sitting down, depending on how it was trained. Then a sample from that area is sent to the lab for scientific testing so the results can be used in a criminal trial. Most of these dogs can recognize about a dozen different accelerants.

🔥 Accelerant-detecting dogs like Smoke, a young Belgian Malinois, are chosen for their intelligence and obedience, as well as their sharp sense of smell. They go through months of training and testing. Smoke used to wear these leather boots to protect his paws against the water-logged debris, but these days he goes barefoot; the boots distracted him (imagine working in a pair of soggy socks), and he's always careful about where he puts his feet down. Dogs are also trained to find bodies, saving many hours of laborious digging through the rubble.

A novel written by a real-life investigator describes the painstaking work of a fire marshal who doesn't believe claims that a certain blaze was started accidentally, by an electrical problem:

He sloshed through the water-logged debris, scraped off char to examine light switches, unscrewed electrical outlets, pried open conduits, and examined circuit-breaker boxes. But no matter where he looked, he couldn't find any tripped circuits, any blown fuses, or any beaded wires.

It takes a while, but the determined fire marshal eventually finds proof that the fire was started on purpose, in three different parts of the building, using an accelerant.

🔥 Investigators go over every inch of a fire scene, looking for the smallest clue. Stopped clocks may show what time the fire reached them. Different burning or melting points may reveal the fire's temperature. For example, aluminum melts at 1,220°F (660°C) and brass melts at 1,724°F (940°C). If the aluminum parts of a lamp have melted but the brass parts haven't, the fire must have been between those two temperatures.

Sometimes the clue to arson is what *isn't* there. Suppose business owners have parked their new car a block away from the building, instead of right in front as usual. Suppose there is no sign of irreplaceable treasures like photo albums and family memorabilia. Suppose a burned-out car is missing its radio and tape deck. Investigators will want to know why these items just happened to be removed before the fire could destroy them. The *modus operandi* (method of working) may also be a tipoff; if there have been other recent fires in similar locations, or set in similar ways, arson is suspected.

If there are bodies in the ruins, the autopsy will probably show whether the victims died in the fire, or were murdered earlier. In one case, investigators found a body charred beyond recognition, and a suicide note in another room. The autopsy revealed not only that the victim had been shot to death, but that he wasn't the man who'd written the note! The note-writer had murdered an acquaintance and substituted the body for his own, hoping to escape and start a new life. Instead he was charged with murder, and later killed himself for real.

Computerized sleuthing

If investigators think they've found traces of accelerant – maybe they smell it, or get a positive reading on a portable detection device – they send samples to a *forensic* (criminal investigation) laboratory. The lab may use *gas-liquid chromatography* and *mass spectrometry* to search out even tiny traces of suspicious

MOVING THE OFFICE TO THE FIRE

American authorities are now developing a "virtual office" that can be taken to the fire. A sturdy portable kit holds a laptop computer, fire-modeling programs, digital and video cameras, a scanner and color printer, a fax and other advanced communications, and a reference library on CD-ROM. It even has built-in batteries in case there's no electricity at the fire site. In the future the kit will have a satellite interface, and software to let investigators build a three-dimensional computer model of the fire scene while they're right there on the spot.

🔥 Forensic technologist Eamonn McGee uses chromatography to separate the components of a mixture. This process can be used to identify substances that might have started a fire, or helped it burn. A tiny liquid or gas sample of the unknown substance is injected into a tube which is heated in the gas chromatograph. A *mobile phase*, such as helium gas, sweeps the sample through a very long, thin tube lined with a *stationary phase* – a liquid that varies, chemically, depending on what's being tested. As the components of the heated sample interact with the stationary phase, some parts move down the tube faster than others. The electrical output from the chromatograph's detector is recorded in a pattern called a *chromatogram*, which shows how long it took each component to pass through the tube. Then the forensic scientist compares the chromatogram to standard test patterns, to identify the material. The sample here shows gasoline, Varsol (paint thinner), and furnace oil. The peaks show the relative amount of each component, and the distance left to right shows how long the component took to exit the tube. To get measurements that are even more detailed, a mass spectrometer is used.

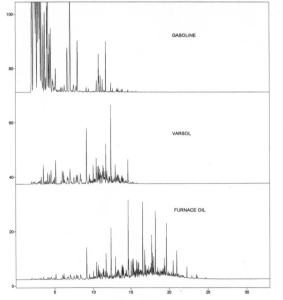

material. Substances can also be tested using infrared or ultraviolet light. If an ordinary microscope doesn't reveal enough detail, a scanning electron microscope can be used to magnify a sample up to 65,000 times. X-ray images can show the insides of things that have melted in the blaze.

Investigators use the Internet to discuss puzzling fires, and to consult technical experts. There are websites with detailed information about building construction, specific flammable materials, and so on. Computer modeling is also becoming a powerful tool: the way the fire really spread can be compared to a computer's prediction of how it should have spread in that kind of building. If the evidence doesn't match the prediction, investigators can run the program again and again, trying various arson patterns on the computer, until they find one that matches the fire.

Meanwhile, the police will be investigating people involved in either the fire or the property. They will pore over insurance claims and financial records. They'll check insurance files to see if this owner has had any other suspicious fires, or any criminal charges. They'll ask about enemies, rivals, anyone else who might have a motive for setting the fire. Once they have a suspect, they can examine the person's belongings for traces of accelerant. Suspects may be asked to take a lie-detector test, or a stress-evaluator test that measures tension in the voice.

Because arson is such a serious and destructive crime, arson investigations are often lengthy, and always painstaking. Police and fire officials work together – often with the help of insurance investigators – to bring to justice anyone who uses fire for criminal purposes.

Try some chromatography at home. You'll need three or four water-soluble (non-permanent) marking pens in different colors, scissors, a paper coffee filter, a kitchen skewer, and a small jar or glass.

The paper is your stationary phase. Cut it in 1-inch (2.5-cm) strips with a V at the bottom, and put a dot of ink about an inch above the bottom. Use a different color for each strip.

Punch the skewer through the top of each strip, so all the strips hang at the same length, without touching each other. Now suspend the skewer over the jar or glass. Don't let the strips touch the sides of the glass.

Water is your mobile phase. Carefully pour a small amount into the glass, without spilling it down the strips. The water should be high enough to touch the end of each strip, but shouldn't touch the ink dot.

Over the next twenty minutes, as the water sweeps the ink sample up the paper, some of the ink's ingredients should travel faster than others. If there's no color separation, it means the ink had only one ingredient. Note that different brands of pen, in the same color, may make different patterns. You can also change the results by changing the phases: use different paper, or substitute rubbing (isopropyl) alcohol for water.

What you've just done is paper chromatography, which is used to analyze different inks. It works on the same principles as gas–liquid chromatography.

CATS IN TREES

Nottinghamshire firefighters answered an emergency call to free a pet goldfish which had become stuck in an ornamental boot inside its bowl. . . .

Norfolk firefighters arrived at a house in King's Lynn to find an Alsatian puppy with its head stuck in the garden wall. . . .

Residents have been turning up their noses at five volunteer firefighters who ended up waist-deep in manure while trying to rescue a pig. . . .

To cope with the various hazards of fire, firefighters have learned over the years to use a wide range of skills and tools. Because they have those skills and tools, they find themselves called out to deal with many non-fire emergencies. In fact, there's just about nothing they haven't been called for. Many fire departments have finally had to draw the line. They no longer roll out their trucks when Fido's hiding in a pipe or Fluffy has run up a tree, because it takes them away from true life-threatening emergencies. Even so, most fire crews now spend far more time on other calls than they do on fires.

🔥 The qualifications listed on this woman's helmet – firefighter, emergency medical technician, hazmat technician – indicate the wide range of skills needed by today's fire crews. Women are gradually making their way into the profession, which was for centuries a male domain.

❡ Firefighters do cardio-pulmonary resuscitation (CPR) on someone whose heart has failed. The rescuer on the right is pumping the heart in an artificial heartbeat while his partner forces oxygen into the victim's lungs. Many fire crews now carry automatic *defibrillators*; paddles placed on the victim's chest send an electric shock through the heart, to try to restore a normal heartbeat.

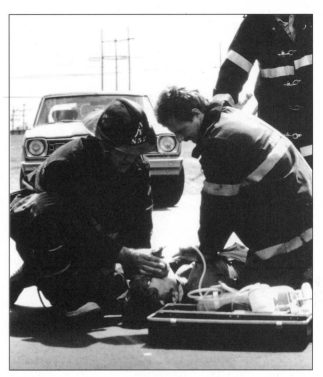

Stopped hearts and broken bones

Since firefighters are trained and equipped to give first aid – and since most communities have more fire trucks than ambulances – crews deal with many medical emergencies. When someone has an accident or is suddenly taken ill, they often reach the scene first, and take charge until medical help arrives. Many firefighters now have advanced training as emergency medical technicians – far beyond basic first aid.

Going into harm's way

Before fire crews can help people, they have to get to them. They force their way into stuck elevators to release captive office workers. They crawl into sewer pipes to cut stuck children free. They retrieve injured window-washers from disabled rigs on skyscrapers, and snatch would-be suicides off bridges. In many areas they also do search-and-rescue duties: they work their ladders over bogs and swamps to drag people out, rappel down cliffs to haul up stranded climbers, lower themselves from helicopters to snatch boaters from the savage undertow of weirs and dams.

🔥 Firefighter Skip Fernandez and his search dog, Aspen, comfort each other. They have just spent a grim twelve-hour shift searching for victims in the rubble of Oklahoma City's Murrah building, blown up by a bomb in 1995.

Perhaps most nerve-racking of all, they burrow into buildings collapsed by earthquakes or bombs. They find trapped victims by using thermal imaging, search dogs, or sensitive noise and motion detectors that pick up the slightest movement. There are even video cameras with fiber-optic lenses mounted on long probes; the probe is inserted into a heap of debris, and the operator can see whether anyone is inside. Crews prop up teetering ruins with airbags, jacks, and timbers, test the air regularly for poisonous and flammable gases, and feel their way through wreckage that could come crashing down at any moment, until they reach the people trapped deep inside.

These are highly skilled jobs that draw on the firefighters' expertise in areas like construction, ropework, and tool use. Physical strength and trust in other team members are essential. But in the end, much of the work comes down to raw courage — and sheer determination not to give up.

❦ While a paramedic gives the driver oxygen and uses a plastic *cervical collar* to support his neck, to avoid damage to his spinal column, a firefighter works to cut away the wrecked car. To keep injured people as safe as possible, rescue crews are taught, "Don't remove the victim from the vehicle; remove the *vehicle* from the *victim*."

Of course, getting in is only part of the job. Beams or chunks of concrete may have to be lifted before people can be pulled out. Victims may be so badly hurt that they can't move. They may need life-saving first aid on the spot; they may have to be maneuvered out in a Stokes litter or on a backboard.

Some of the most difficult extrications are from vehicles. Cars are designed to be strong enough to protect us in a crash, but all that steel can become a trap holding someone inside. Doors jam shut, the roof buckles, the steering wheel pins the driver in place. Fire crews may work for an hour or more with extrication tools, prying and cutting their way through the tangled mass.

INCH BY INCH

In 1986, a deep construction trench collapsed and left a man named Patrick Kelly buried waist-deep. Kelly's coworkers couldn't pull him free, and they were afraid the top of the trench might fall in and bury his head. Fire crews were called and began cautiously digging the soil out by hand, carting it away by bucket brigade. When they found a huge boulder buried beside him, they rigged slings around it so it couldn't roll onto him. When they found his pneumatic drill jammed against his legs, they hacksawed through the compressor pipe and carefully extracted the drill. Laboring in the narrow trench – sometimes working almost upside down – they gradually freed Kelly, worked a harness around him, and used a vehicle to draw him up to a waiting ambulance crew. The rescue had taken over two hours of patient, painstaking effort; with more speed and less expertise, crews might not have got Kelly out alive.

Leaks and spills

Many emergencies – earth-quakes, explosions, truck or train collisions, industrial accidents, airplane crashes – are complicated by the presence of hazardous materials. These may be flammable or explosive. They may be *corrosives* (poisons that eat through skin and fabric), or toxins that poison us if we touch, taste, or breathe them. They may be radioactive, or *biohazardous* – that is, disease-spreading, such as hospital waste. If they're liquid, hose water or normal firefighting foam may only wash them over a wider area, or flush them into the water supply. If they give off gas or mist, they can disperse quickly into crowded areas.

🔥 Protected by an encapsulating suit, a firefighter uses a "sniffer" device to identify fumes, to see if they are poisonous or explosive.

There are strict rules about storing and transporting hazmat. Once fire crews know what they are dealing with, they can decide on the safest way to contain the mess and clean it up. They wear all-over protective suits that prevent any contact at all with the dangerous substance. They can use special foams to blanket certain materials so they don't spread poisonous fumes. Some pollutants can be safely burned away; others can be soaked up by absorbent mats or pillows, or trapped by dams of piled-up earth. Some can be neutralized, absorbed, or curdled into solids by the right chemicals.

Too often, dangerous materials are moved and stored illegally, and even secretly dumped, by people who don't bother about safety. Discovering the risk, and then identifying the material, can be difficult and time-consuming. Fortunately, computerized portable detectors can pick out many products by analyzing their ingredients.

🔥 An engine crew rescues a man trapped in his truck by summer floods. The maneuver was trickier than it looks. "If we didn't keep a steady speed," Captain Rusty Ross explained later, "water would have gotten into our tailpipe and stalled the engine." Perhaps that's how the truck got stuck in the first place.

Swift-water rescues

When heavy rains or the spring thaw bring flooding, rivers, valleys, and even towns can turn into seething waterways. Often residents are taken by surprise, or refuse to believe that they're really in danger. They insist on staying in their homes for "just one more night," or driving their cars through flooded streets. Suddenly they find themselves stranded on the house roof, or in the car, or even clinging to a tree – anywhere they can stay above the sucking floodwaters.

Swift-water rescue teams wear special flotation vests, and often diving suits as well, to keep out the water's deathly chill. They use ropes handled by partners on shore, with an assortment of knots and attachments, to ensure their own safety and to haul themselves out to the victims. Sometimes they use rescue boats connected by ropes, so that one boat keeps the other from being sucked into danger. One ingenious trick is to pump a fire hose full of air so it floats like a giant pool toy, and push it out to the victim. Meanwhile, ambulance crews stand by, ready to assist both the victims and the rescuers.

As winter snows melt and creeks and rivers rise, the water may not look very dangerous. But a current of just 12 miles (20 km) an hour has a force of 538 pounds (244 kg) – impossible for any swimmer to resist – and rocks and tree trunks in the river make the rushing water even more deadly. Would-be rescuers who tie themselves to something on shore are simply pulled off their feet and drowned. Rescuing people out of fast-moving water is a complex, dangerous job that takes a lot of training and teamwork. It's no wonder that, when untrained people attempt it, they often become victims themselves.

Danger, thin ice!

Too many people assume that ice is simple stuff – just frozen water, right? In fact, ice goes through different stages as the temperature rises and falls, and it can be very unpredictable. Somebody ventures out on a surface that's mostly frozen solid, hits one weak patch, and plunges into water that's numbingly cold.

🔥 Firefighters wearing *drysuits* (waterproof diving suits) practice ice rescue techniques. A safety line (held by partners not in the picture) is attached to the rescuer's harness and looped around the victim. People usually fall through weak patches of ice that aren't obvious, but as they struggle to escape they create a big hole like this one. In a real rescue the victim would probably be too cold to hold onto anything, and might even be unconscious.

Soon the victim is too cold to hang on, let alone climb out. Then confusion and sleepiness set in, and finally unconsciousness.

Some search-and-rescue teams have airboats or hovercraft that can skim over the ice to reach the freezing victim. Most teams have to get themselves out there the old-fashioned way, using ladders or special rescue boards to spread their weight over the ice. Using their knowledge of ropes and rock-climbing gear, they create a lifeline for themselves and the victims. Years of experience have taught them: "No ice is safe ice."

◊ For the movie *Blackjack*, a stuntman standing in for star Dolph Lundgren flees a mansion as it explodes in a giant fireball. The film crew rented a real house, but built a false back onto it, to create this elegant disaster. Although special effects like this are worked out by experts, there's always the slight possibility of something going wrong.

🔥 Alan Sutton (left) and a colleague from 1st Unit Fire & Safety check the *Blackjack* set after the fire. Although the company works in Toronto, it has turnout gear from many cities and from as far back as the 1950s. It also has stacks of magnetic signs to transform its fire trucks; the engine that says "Chicago" this month may have said "New York" last month, and "Los Angeles" the month before that!

Lights, cameras, extinguishers!

When you watch an action movie where everything is bursting into flame and smoke, do you ever wonder how the actors stay safe? The explosions, sheets of flame, and billows of smoke are created by special-effects experts, but fire has a way of getting out of hand. That's why special film-firefighters are usually nearby, ready to take over. If a scene is being filmed several times, they may be asked to douse the flames between takes – and they have to do it without damaging expensive sets and props. If something goes seriously wrong, they can move in and deal with it instantly. As well, they keep an eye on fire safety, and act as consultants. Sometimes they are even hired as actors – to play firefighters!

Alan Sutton, a firefighter who has worked on many movies and television shows, points out that film work sometimes goes against a firefighter's instincts. "On set, you have to wait for the full shot, unless you see something dangerous. It's tough to see something burning and have to stand back, because you really want to go in and put out that fire!"

TAMING THE TIGER

To people long ago, fire was a mystery – perhaps a god, perhaps a tool of the devil. To us, it's more like a member of the family. As candles on the dining room table, smoldering coals in the barbecue, or a furnace roaring in the basement, this age-old companion still brings us heat, light, and comfort.

These days, though, we use electricity for most of our needs. It's cleaner and safer. It's a lot more convenient: no woodpiles, no ashes, no matches and kindling – just flip a switch and there it is. But electricity is first cousin to fire. If we're careless about how we use it, or how we control it, we may find ourselves face to face with its ancient relative.

Think of the "tiger" of fire that guarded the cave entrance so many thousands of years ago. We have brought that tiger into our homes, first as fire and then as electricity. We've made it our servant; we like to think it's tame. But the truth is, it's still a tiger. Like the tiger-keeper at the zoo, we need to understand the beast we're dealing with. We need to know what we're doing – what's safe and what isn't. And we *always* need to know how to escape if we need to.

🔥 During a safety-training session, Steve McCabe guides Abigail Ostrowski through the steps of making an emergency call: stay calm, give your name and location, answer all the dispatcher's questions, don't hang up until the dispatcher does. Do you know your local emergency phone number?

What about all those fire precautions?

Fire-prevention measures protect us only if we respect them. Too many people don't. They block off emergency fire exits, or prop open fire doors that are supposed to hold back deadly smoke. They park their cars in fire access lanes. They plug too many appliances into their electrical wiring, and deliberately bypass the fuses that are meant to keep electrical circuits from being overloaded. They disable smoke detectors, or don't bother to replace the dead batteries.

If you see violations of the fire code like these, you can report them to someone responsible. There are also many ways you can take charge of your own fire safety.

PREVENTION – AND SIMPLE COMMON SENSE

- Keep matches and lighters away from children.
- If anyone smokes, use large, safe ashtrays, and empty them into non-flammable containers. Never let people smoke in bed, or anywhere they are likely to doze off.
- Don't wear flammable materials, even for party costumes.
- Keep anything flammable at least 4 feet (1.2 m) away from heat sources (stoves, water heaters, clothes dryers, etc.). Never dry clothes on a room heater.
- When you use an appliance, follow the manufacturer's instructions. As far as possible, turn off appliances when you go to bed or leave the house.
- If an appliance is smoking or smells hot, unplug it right away, and don't use it until it's repaired.
- If you use room heaters, be sure they can't tip over, and keep them 3 feet (1 meter) from drapes and furniture.
- Be sure lamps can't tip, too. If you have halogen lamps, make sure they have shields; these lamps get very hot and can be a major fire hazard.
- Keep fireplaces safely screened, with no flammable materials too close.
- Don't wear loose, long-sleeved clothing around a stove. Fasten long hair safely out of the way.
- Keep young children away from stoves and other hot appliances.
- Keep a fire extinguisher in the kitchen, for putting out small fires, but don't use it on burning oil; you may just splash the fire around.
- If a pan of cooking oil catches fire, don't try to move it. Put a tight-fitting lid on the pan to cut off the oxygen, and turn off the heat.
- Use extension cords only as a temporary measure, and don't plug too many appliances into one outlet.
- Give your Christmas tree lots of water so it doesn't dry out, and don't put anything hot near the tree. Turn off tree lights when you go out or go to bed, and never use real candles on a tree.

When you go to a public building – a movie theater, say – take a moment to look for the exits. Would you be able to get to them? Where are the telephones and fire alarms? You don't have to be obsessed with fire safety. You just need to remember that fires do happen, and that common sense saves lives.

What about at home?

Fire safety at home comes down to prevention, detection, and preparation. Prevention includes a long, long list of precautions, but it really means thinking about what you're doing, and asking yourself, "What if . . . ?" When you notice an electrical cord worn bare, ask yourself, "What would happen if that wire got too hot, lying on the carpet like that?" If the phone rings when you're using the stove, ask yourself, "What would happen if I got talking and forgot the stove was on?"

WHY DO PEOPLE IGNORE FIRE ALARMS?

Dr. Guylene Proulx is a researcher studying people's reactions to fire. She's trying to understand why so many people stay in a building after a fire alarm goes off. One reason is that they don't realize how fast a blaze can spread. "In a fire you have a limited time to get out safely – maybe two or three minutes," she says. "They think they have plenty of time, perhaps ten to fifteen minutes, to escape." A second reason is that people have heard so many false alarms. In one fire in a high-rise apartment building, only 18 percent of the residents took the alarm seriously; the others peered out the windows for fire trucks, consulted their neighbors, or just waited for news. As a result, six people died. A third reason, in a public place like an arena, is that everybody waits for someone else to make a decision; we all feel embarrassed about going first. If you feel this way, go first anyway; this is one time when you really can "die of embarrassment"!

ᨒ When can you use a fire extinguisher? Only when

ᨒ the fire is small;

ᨒ you are not in danger;

ᨒ everyone else is leaving the building;

ᨒ the fire department has been called; and

ᨒ you have the right kind of extinguisher (A for ordinary fires like paper and wood, B for flammable gas fires, and C for electrical fires. An ABC extinguisher can be used for any of these).

Store your extinguisher in plain view, and where it's handy – preferably near the exit. Know how to take it off its storage mount. Read the instructions ahead of time, and make sure you understand them.

To use the extinguisher:

ᨒ remove it from its storage mount;

ᨒ pull out the locking pin, breaking the seal (you may have to release a latch);

ᨒ standing about 10 feet (3 m) away, aim the hose or nozzle at the base of the fire;

ᨒ squeeze the trigger handle all the way, to fire the extinguisher; and

ᨒ sweep the nozzle from side to side, advancing from the front of the fire to the back as you put the fire out. Keep your eyes on the fire area, even when you think the fire is out.

To remember the steps, use the acronym PASS:

ᨒ Pull the pin;

ᨒ Aim at the base of the fire;

ᨒ Squeeze the handle;

ᨒ Sweep the nozzle from side to side.

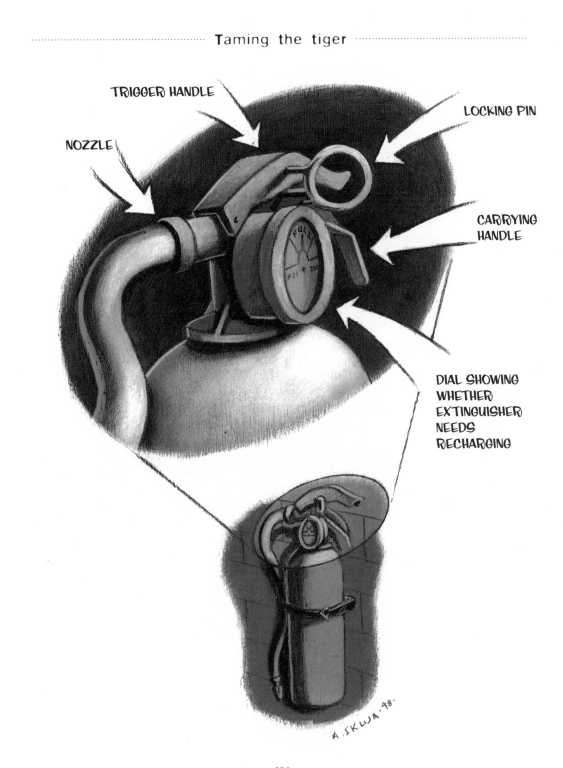

TRIGGER HANDLE

NOZZLE

LOCKING PIN

CARRYING HANDLE

DIAL SHOWING WHETHER EXTINGUISHER NEEDS RECHARGING

A. SKUJA. '98.

In a home, the main fire-detecting tool is the smoke alarm. If something starts burning in the daytime, when you're awake, there's a good chance you'll smell it in time to escape. When people are sleeping, though, smoke and poisonous gases can spread without being noticed. You should have a smoke alarm on every level of your home, even the basement. There should be one outside every sleeping area. If you sleep with the door closed, you need an alarm inside the bedroom. Alarms should be placed on the ceiling, because smoke rises. They should be tested regularly (follow the manufacturer's instructions), and any batteries should be replaced at least once a year.

Be prepared!

Preparation means knowing what to do in a fire. It also means practicing, to be sure your plan will work, and to give you experience so you won't panic and

🔥 Stuart Henderson answers Anja Kovacevic's question during a school visit. Firefighters work hard at educating people about how to prevent fires, and what to do in a fire. They know what it's like inside a burning building; they don't want you to find out the hard way.

Dalmatians have been firehouse dogs since the years when pumper engines were pulled by horses. As hunting dogs they had been bred to work with horses, so they could run in front of the engines and clear people off the road. They are also very protective of their "territory"; they are still sometimes used to guard the engine while the crew are busy with the fire, or to stay home and protect the deserted fire hall. Firehouse dalmatians are traditionally named Sparky – maybe because they look as though they've stood a little too close to a fire.

forget what to do. You need to know how to get out of the building, and what to do if you can't get out. (If you're a babysitter, you need to know your way out of your customers' homes too!)

Sometimes people can put out small fires by themselves; sometimes they have time to phone for help before they leave. But all too often, they delay getting out until it's too late. Unless you are *absolutely positive* you have time to do more, just get people out, and call for help from a neighbor's house, or on a cellular phone. And don't stop to get properly dressed, to hunt for a wallet or purse, or to find an elusive cat or dog. Many, many people have died trying to save a pet. Anyway, animals aren't dummies; most of them find their own way out.

What's that funny smell?

Imagine you're alone in your apartment, halfway through your homework, when you smell something weird. You trace the smell to the living room, and there you find the drapes blazing, and the flames spreading to the couch. What should you do?

You think of the fire extinguisher out in the hall – but it's not very big, and it probably won't put out the fire. You'd better get out while there's still time. You shut the living room door, to cut down the air supply and hold back the smoke. Then you leave the apartment and close the door behind you. You shout, "FIRE! FIRE!" as loud as you can. Nothing happens; most people aren't home yet. But some people are, and you want to warn them. As you go to the nearest fire alarm, you remember all the times you've been told never, never to touch it – but right there on the box it says, "In case of fire break glass," and this sure is a fire, so here goes. . . .

SNAP! The glass breaks and the alarm bell drills through your eardrums. You head for the stairs, but just then a door opens and Mrs. Green sticks her head out. You forgot all about her – she's pretty deaf, she wouldn't have heard you shouting. You tell her there's a fire, and she pops back into her apartment. What's the matter with her? Doesn't she believe you? What are you supposed to do now? But in a moment she's back, carrying her purse and heading for the elevator. She shouldn't have gone back for that purse!

"We have to use the stairs, Mrs. Green," you say. "If the elevator stops, we could be stuck in the smoke."

"Stairs?" she says. "Oh dear, I can't – well, all right, but can you stay with me? I'm not too good on stairs these days." As the two of you climb slowly down the stairwell, you hear footsteps clattering below. Good – that means people are getting out, and not just sitting around thinking about it. You wonder if any of them have portable phones, to call the fire department. You strain your ears for the sound of sirens.

At last you come out through the lobby into fresh air. Other tenants are milling about and grumbling – you hear "false alarm" and "kids fooling around" – but you can also hear sirens, and they're pretty close. Just as you get Mrs. Green to a ledge where she can sit down, a police cruiser wheels up. A pumper engine and ladder truck scream around the corner, with an ambulance not far behind. As you explain what happened, firefighters are already grabbing their gear and hurrying inside. You have a feeling of relief so strong you're almost floating. *They're going to fix it. They're going to put out the fire. It's not your problem any more.*

What if the fire is somewhere else in the building?

When you think there may be a fire – perhaps you hear an alarm, or smell smoke – get to safety if you can; but *think* about what you're doing. If you panic and run for the door, you may put yourself in worse danger. If you're

THE BOY WHO PLAYED WITH MATCHES

When Pascal Thibodeau was three years old, he decided to sit in the family car and play with matches. His pajamas caught fire, and so did the car seat. He was badly burned by the time a neighbor rushed out and smothered the flames with a blanket.

The little boy spent two months in hospital, and had medical treatment almost every day for the next six years, including fifteen serious operations and many painful procedures. He spent his childhood wearing gloves and a face mask to protect his damaged skin. "My life was shaped by pain, both physical and social," he says. "I didn't even want to go outside because of the mask."

Pascal Thibodeau is now twenty-seven. He is badly scarred, and he still needs more surgery, but through enormous effort and courage he has built a normal life – in fact, he wants to be a firefighter. After all, he knows better than anyone how terrible the results of a fire can be.

🔥 Steve McCabe and Chris Ogilvie help Robert McLeod (top) and David Smith escape from a "burning building" – a two-story trailer that visits local schools. When the alarm sounds, students stay calm, crawl through mock smoke, climb down to safety, and assemble at a meeting point. Chris (left) is a high school student taking part in a work experience program; he hopes to become a real firefighter.

leaving an apartment or hotel room, take the key with you, in case you can't escape the building and you decide to go back to your room. Feel the door-knob before you go out; if it's hot, *don't open the door*. If the knob feels cool, open the door cautiously, go to the stairwell, and test that door. If the door feels cool but the stairwell is full of smoke, *don't go in*; look for another exit. And don't be tempted to flee to the roof. That would just put you farther from rescue – right up there with all that rising smoke.

Once you reach safety, be sure to tell the firefighters you're out, so they don't have to keep looking for you. *Never, never go back into a burning building.*

If you aren't able to get out, try to make a safe refuge in your own apart-ment. Close the doors to keep the smoke out, and seal the cracks with tape or wet towels. If the phone is working, call the emergency number and tell the dispatcher exactly where you are. Don't assume that the fire department has already been called.

Go out on the balcony, if there is one. If not, go to the room farthest from the smoke, and try to hang a sheet or towel out the window, to show where you are. (Don't hide in a closet or under a bed, or the firefighters may not find you.) Stay close to the ground, below the smoke, and use a damp towel as a mask against the smoke. Make yourself stay calm. Of course it's scary to be in a building that's on fire. But you know that a lot of very brave, very experienced rescuers are on their way to get you out. It may take a while; they have a job to do, and they have to do it right. You can help them by using your own knowledge to stay safe until they reach you.

Have your own family fire drill

Public buildings like offices and schools often have fire drills so everybody can practice getting outside. But what about your home? What if you woke up in bed, or in front of the TV, in thick smoke? Could you feel your way out on your hands and knees? What if the only stairway was blocked; could you get out a window or onto a balcony? Could you get that window or balcony door open in the dark? If you're on a lower level of the building, is there some way you could reach the ground safely? If you're in a big building, do you know how many doors you have to crawl past to reach the fire exit? You should know two ways out of every room in your home, and you should know your way out with your eyes shut.

You can practice this – and have some fun at the same time – by holding a family fire drill twice a year. If you live in a house, you may be able to make your practice more realistic by setting off the fire alarm, so your brain learns to connect that noise with danger. Let people take turns crawling out of various rooms with their eyes shut. Try confusing them by closing a door, or moving a chair, or telling them the route they've chosen is blocked by the fire. (Watch where they're going, of course, so nobody gets hurt.) You'll soon get used to feeling your way around, and you'll get a sense of how long it takes you to crawl from one place to another. And if you ever have to escape in a real fire, you'll be less likely to panic. You'll be able to tell yourself, *I know I can do this, because I've done it before.*

Your fire drill should include an outdoor meeting place. In a real fire, you'd want to get together and count heads, to be sure everybody was safely out.

What if somebody's clothing is on fire?

If your clothes catch fire, the magic words are "Stop, drop, and roll." That means don't panic or run, and don't slap frantically at the flames; just drop to the ground, put your hands over your face, and roll over and over until the fire is out. If someone else's clothes catch fire, you can tell the person to stop, drop, and roll – or you can smother the fire by throwing a heavy coat, blanket, or rug over the person. (Most people know they should stop, drop, and roll, but in their panic they may forget.)

❧ When Tara Perry was eleven, she and her friends were playing with sparklers, and Tara's clothes caught fire. As the heat seared her back, Tara remembered the magic words; she stopped, dropped to the ground, and rolled and rolled until the flames were out. Tara had severe burns and had to spend time in hospital, but thanks to her training and quick thinking she recovered fully. Now fifteen, Tara says, "Never panic in a fire. Just think clearly and remember your fire safety."

Even in this age of science, when we can build a computer on a pinhead and slice up genetic material like so much sausage, fire remains one of our most amazing and versatile tools. We can use it to shape tons of raw material into a space shuttle and launch it toward the stars – or to turn a rubbery pellet of marshmallow into a treat so good it's almost wicked. There's just one rule in dealing with this powerful, magical servant: we have to treat it with respect.

Doesn't it deserve that much?

FIRST AID FOR FIRE INJURIES

First aid for burns

- Cool the burn with cold water (not ice water) *right away*.
- Burned skin will swell, so take off anything tight (rings, watches) before the swelling starts. But *don't* pull off anything that's already sticking to the burn.
- If the skin is broken, or if you need to protect the burn, tape on a clean dressing that won't leave lint. Be sure none of the tape touches the burn. (Use a commercial "burn dressing" if you have one. Burn dressings are made of water jelly so they can't stick. Most drugstores sell them.) Avoid greasy oils and ointments.
- Unless the burn is minor, a doctor should check it – especially if the person burned is a small child or elderly, or if the burn is on a place that's hard to keep clean (like a foot). Never break the blisters on a burn. Burns get infected very easily, so it's important to keep them clean.

First aid for smoke inhalation

What if people breathe in smoke or poisonous gases from a fire? First they need fresh air, either through a window or outdoors. If they're unconscious, you may have to drag them outside. Then they need medical attention, even if they feel all right. If their lungs have been damaged by the heat and gas, they may develop breathing problems a little later.

If the smoke and gas have stopped someone's breathing, or stopped the heart from beating, you need the first-aid techniques of mouth-to-mouth breathing and CPR. If you don't learn these in school, you can take courses from community colleges and first-aid training agencies. These skills can also help you get part-time and summer jobs.

SOURCE NOTES

Where no reference is supplied for a quotation, the remark was made during discussion with the author.

"Put the wet stuff on the red stuff"

The Toronto fire regulations are cited in *A History of the Toronto Fire Department* (Toronto: Toronto Fire Department, n.d.). The verse is from *Scribner's* magazine, Library of Congress, Prints and Photographs Division, LC-USZ62-58630. The description of the fire is from *The News* (Toronto, April 20, 1904), and is cited in *The Great Toronto Fire* by Nancy Rawson and Richard Tatton (Erin, Ontario: Boston Mills, 1984).

Beating the "Red Devil"

The stories of the rugby match and the sheep costumes are recounted in *The Real Blue Watch* by Geoff Tibballs (London: Virgin, 1996).

"Fire, fire, fire!"

The Luc Thibault quote is from "Vision Looks to Cut Emergency Response Time," by Linda Stuart, in *Computerworld Canada*, June 21, 1996. The Leo

Stapleton quote is from "Fire!," an episode of CBS Television's series *Real America: 48 Hours*. The quotes from Frank Lawrence and Eddie Munroe are from "Firefighting," a program on The Learning Channel featuring firefighters in South Boston. The anonymous quote "You're gonna take a beating" is from *The Fire Inside: Firefighters Talk about Their Lives* by Steve Delsohn (New York: HarperCollins, 1996).

Wildfire!

The quotes from Doug Houston and Mike Stebbing are from "Into the Fray," an episode of the TV series *Danger Zone* on The Learning Channel. The remarks about the fire shelter are cited in *The Fire Inside*.

Ships, Planes, and Subway Trains

The Herb Morrison quote is cited in *Lighter Than Air: An Illustrated History of the Airship* by Lee Payne (New York: Orion, 1977). The description of the *Noronic* fire is based on an account by Marla Friebe of the Toronto Fire Department. The account of the London Underground fire is drawn from *The Real Blue Watch*. The computerized oil-rig simulator is at Montrose Fire and Emergency Training Centre in Scotland. The account is based on "Feeling the Heat," in *The Economist*, July 5, 1997. The Ouellette quote is cited in *Flame of Courage* by Allan de la Plante (Etobicoke, Ontario: Window, 1993).

Playing with Fire

The Jack Carney quote is from *Heat: The Fire Investigators and Their War on Arson and Murder* by Peter A. Micheels (New York: St. Martin's, 1991). The comments on the characteristics of firebugs are drawn from *Fire and Fire-Raisers* by Donald Scott (London: Duckworth, 1974), and *Bombers and Firesetters* by John M. MacDonald (Springfield, Illinois: Charles C. Thomas, 1977); the quote from the firebug, and the story of the murderous "suicide," are from the latter. The story of the suspicious fire marshal is from *Origin and Cause* by Shelley Reuben

(New York: Scribner's, 1994). The remarks on the significance of glass are drawn from "Glass and Fire Cause Determination," by Peter Heyerhoff, in *Ontario Fire Service Messenger*, July/August 1993. The chromatography experiment is based on "Gas Chromatography," by Margaret A. and Craig A. Balliets, in *Fire Findings*, spring 1996. The description of the virtual office (transportable rapid information package, or TRIP) is based on "USFA and U.S. TVA Police Interagency Partnerships," in *NFPA Journal*, May/June 1997.

Cats in Trees

In the chapter opening, the goldfish and puppy rescues are quoted from *The Real Blue Watch*, and the pig story (from Carberry, Manitoba) is quoted from *The Globe and Mail*, July 6, 1998. The story of Patrick Kelly is also drawn from *The Real Blue Watch*. The Rusty Ross quote is from *Rescue*, November/December 1996. The Alan Sutton quote is from "Meet the Guys Who Take the Film-Biz Heat," by Rita Zekas, in *The Toronto Star*, December 28, 1997.

Taming the Tiger

The material about Dr. Proulx is drawn from "Fire and the Human Psyche," by Ray Ford, in *The Globe and Mail*, February 7, 1998. The story of Pascal Thibodeau is from "What I Remember Most Is the Pain," by André Picard, in *The Globe and Mail*, October 1, 1997.

PICTURE SOURCES

Every reasonable effort has been made to trace the ownership of copyright materials. Any information allowing the publisher to correct a reference or credit in future will be welcomed. Pictures not attributed are from the author's collection.

For space reasons the following abbreviations have been used:

FD   Fire Department (generally)
LC   Library of Congress (Washington)
NYFD   North York Fire Department (Toronto)
TFS   Toronto Fire Services
USDA   Forest Services, United States Dept. of Agriculture

Page ii: J. Rankin/*Toronto Star* 95-05-13-16-28; 5, 6: © copyright The British Museum; 9: Musée Guimet, Paris, MG 17 866, photo © copyright RMN; 14, 17: © copyright Guildhall Library, Corporation of London, C 46.61 T 1974, A372/8 p. 1666; 19: Picture Collection, The Branch Libraries, The New York Public Library; 20: Smithsonian Institution, MHT 32515; 21: LC USZ62-25570;

ACKNOWLEDGMENTS

I am deeply grateful to the many people who helped me with this book, sharing their knowledge, their experiences, and even their photographs. Particularly helpful were staff at the North York Fire Department, the Ontario Fire College, the Ontario Fire Marshal's Office, the Toronto Fire Department, and the United States Department of Agriculture, Forestry Services. Special thanks to my editor, Beverley Endersby, and to Kathy Lowinger, publisher of Tundra Books, for not thinking – or at least not saying – that it's time I started acting my age.

INDEX